Property Of:
Oyster River Middle
School

W9-BSF-171

**INTRODUCING
ISSUES WITH
OPPOSING
VIEWPOINTS®**

Media
Violence

Noël Merino, *Book Editor*

GREENHAVEN PRESS
A part of Gale, Cengage Learning

GALE
CENGAGE Learning™

Detroit • New York • San Francisco • New Haven, Conn • Waterville, Maine • London

GALE
CENGAGE Learning

Christine Nasso, *Publisher*
Elizabeth Des Chenes, *Managing Editor*

© 2011 Greenhaven Press, a part of Gale, Cengage Learning

Gale and Greenhaven Press are registered trademarks used herein under license.

For more information, contact:
Greenhaven Press
27500 Drake Rd.
Farmington Hills, MI 48331-3535
Or you can visit our Internet site at gale.cengage.com

For product information and technology assistance, contact us at

Gale Customer Support, 1-800-877-4253
For permission to use material from this text or product, submit all requests online at www.cengage.com/permissions

Further permissions questions can be e-mailed to permissionrequest@cengage.com

Articles in Greenhaven Press anthologies are often edited for length to meet page require-ments. In addition, original titles of these works are changed to clearly present the main thesis and to explicitly indicate the author's opinion. Every effort is made to ensure that Greenhaven Press accurately reflects the original intent of the authors. Every effort has been made to trace the owners of copyrighted material.

Cover image copyright Charles Knox, 2010. Used under license from Shutterstock.com.

LIBRARY OF CONGRESS CATALOGING-IN-PUBLICATION DATA

Media violence / Noël Merino, book editor.
    p. cm. -- (Introducing issues with opposing viewpoints)
  Includes bibliographical references and index.
  ISBN 978-0-7377-4480-4 (hardcover)
  1. Violence in mass media--Juvenile literature. 2. Mass media and children--Juvenile literature. I. Merino, Noël.
  P96.V5M427 2010
  303.6--dc22

                                       2010016978

Printed in the United States of America
1 2 3 4 5 6 7 14 13 12 11 10

Contents

Chapter 3: Should the Government Regulate Violent Media?

Foreword

Indulging in a wide spectrum of ideas, beliefs, and perspectives is a critical cornerstone of democracy. After all, it is often debates over differences of opinion, such as whether to legalize abortion, how to treat prisoners, or when to enact the death penalty, that shape our society and drive it forward. Such diversity of thought is frequently regarded as the hallmark of a healthy and civilized culture. As the Reverend Clifford Schutjer of the First Congregational Church in Mansfield, Ohio, declared in a 2001 sermon, "Surrounding oneself with only like-minded people, restricting what we listen to or read only to what we find agreeable is irresponsible. Refusing to entertain doubts once we make up our minds is a subtle but deadly form of arrogance." With this advice in mind, Introducing Issues with Opposing Viewpoints books aim to open readers' minds to the critically divergent views that comprise our world's most important debates.

Introducing Issues with Opposing Viewpoints simplifies for students the enormous and often overwhelming mass of material now available via print and electronic media. Collected in every volume is an array of opinions that captures the essence of a particular controversy or topic. Introducing Issues with Opposing Viewpoints books embody the spirit of nineteenth-century journalist Charles A. Dana's axiom: "Fight for your opinions, but do not believe that they contain the whole truth, or the only truth." Absorbing such contrasting opinions teaches students to analyze the strength of an argument and compare it to its opposition. From this process readers can inform and strengthen their own opinions, or be exposed to new information that will change their minds. Introducing Issues with Opposing Viewpoints is a mosaic of different voices. The authors are statesmen, pundits, academics, journalists, corporations, and ordinary people who have felt compelled to share their experiences and ideas in a public forum. Their words have been collected from newspapers, journals, books, speeches, interviews, and the Internet, the fastest growing body of opinionated material in the world.

Introducing Issues with Opposing Viewpoints shares many of the well-known features of its critically acclaimed parent series, Opposing Viewpoints. The articles are presented in a pro/con format, allowing readers to absorb divergent perspectives side by side. Active reading questions preface each viewpoint, requiring the student to approach the material thoughtfully and carefully. Useful charts, graphs, and cartoons supplement each article. A thorough introduction provides readers with crucial background on an issue. An annotated bibliography points the reader toward articles, books, and Web sites that contain additional information on the topic. An appendix of organizations to contact contains a wide variety of charities, nonprofit organizations, political groups, and private enterprises that each hold a position on the issue at hand. Finally, a comprehensive index allows readers to locate content quickly and efficiently.

Introducing Issues with Opposing Viewpoints is also significantly different from Opposing Viewpoints. As the series title implies, its presentation will help introduce students to the concept of opposing viewpoints and learn to use this material to aid in critical writing and debate. The series' four-color, accessible format makes the books attractive and inviting to readers of all levels. In addition, each viewpoint has been carefully edited to maximize a reader's understanding of the content. Short but thorough viewpoints capture the essence of an argument. A substantial, thought-provoking essay question placed at the end of each viewpoint asks the student to further investigate the issues raised in the viewpoint, compare and contrast two authors' arguments, or consider how one might go about forming an opinion on the topic at hand. Each viewpoint contains sidebars that include at-a-glance information and handy statistics. A Facts About section located in the back of the book further supplies students with relevant facts and figures.

Following in the tradition of the Opposing Viewpoints series, Greenhaven Press continues to provide readers with invaluable exposure to the controversial issues that shape our world. As John Stuart Mill once wrote: "The only way in which a human being can make some approach to knowing the whole of a subject is by hearing what can be said about it by persons of every variety of opinion and studying all modes in which it can be looked at by every character of mind. No wise man ever acquired his wisdom in any mode but this." It is to this principle that Introducing Issues with Opposing Viewpoints books are dedicated.

Introduction

"Have you not noticed that imitations, if they last from youth for some time, become part of one's nature and settle into the habits of gesture, voice, and thought?"

—Plato, *Republic*

The debate about media violence is one with a long history. Central to the debate is whether watching portrayals of violence encourages people to commit real acts of violence. The main target of this concern has always been the young and impressionable: children. This concern about the impressionability and potential corruptibility of youth goes back to times long before the existence of television, movies, video games, and computers. Today experts continue to discuss how these new technologies have impacted this age-old debate.

Written in the fourth century B.C., Plato's *Republic* disapproves of dramatic poetry, or plays, due to a concern that people—especially youth—will want to imitate morally corrupt characters. Ancient philosophy scholar and Princeton University professor Alexander Nehamas notes how similar Plato's views are to our modern-day concerns about the potentially damaging effects of television, movies, and other media. Nehamas calls for us to be wary of dire warnings about today's media if we think that Plato's concern about dramatic poetry was misguided: "If, then, we think that Plato was wrong to banish dramatic poetry from his city, we must be careful with our own attitude toward the popular entertainment of today."[1] The social concern about people imitating art and about the appropriateness of protecting people from dangerous representations goes back centuries.

Dramatic poetry may seem quite a bit different from today's various media offerings, but the concerns of the modern era are similar to those of Plato's time. The specific concern about violence in media is that viewing depictions of violence will make people, especially young people, more likely to act violently in real life. This concern about the link between media violence and actually violent behavior has spawned congressional hearings and research for several decades in the United States, yet there still appears to be no broad agreement on whether a link can be made.

Well before the advanced technology of the twenty-first century made television, movies, and video games widely available through many devices, there was concern in the United States about the violence in comic books. In 1953 the U.S. Senate created the Judiciary Subcommittee on Juvenile Delinquency to examine potential causes of juvenile crime and antisocial behavior. The subcommittee's hearings in 1954 focused on crime-filled comic books of the day. During those hearings psychiatrist Frederic Wertham testified on his views about the link between violent comics and juvenile delinquency: "It is my opinion, without any reasonable doubt, and without any reservation, that comic books are an important contributing factor in many cases of juvenile delinquency."[2] This statement contrasted with the testimony of publisher William M. Gaines, who stated, "Entertaining reading has never harmed anyone."[3] Despite the disagreement about the effects of violent comics, the hearings resulted in a public outcry. In response to that outcry, and in an attempt to avoid government regulation, the self-regulatory body of comic books, the Comics Magazine Association of America, adopted the Comics Code Authority (CCA). The CCA screened comics for compliance with the code, putting a seal of approval on comics that avoided depictions of graphic violence and sexual content. As a result of the 1954 hearings, the content of comic books changed without any official government regulation.

The debate about television violence has been ongoing since the 1950s, when the first congressional hearings on the issue occurred. In 1972 the surgeon general's office published a report on the link between television violence and aggressive behavior, claiming a link between the two: "We can tentatively conclude that there is a modest relationship between exposure to television violence and aggressive behavior or tendencies."[4] Yet even the surgeon general's report failed to resolve the debate. Instead, it spawned many critics who vocally dismissed the notion of any such link. As readers will see from the viewpoints in *Introducing Issues with Opposing Viewpoints: Media Violence*, this particular debate continues today.

Notes

1. Alexander Nehamas, "Culture, Art, and Poetry in *The Republic*," Fall 1999. www.college.columbia.edu/core/lectures/fall1999.

2. Quoted in TheComicBooks.com, "Testimony of Dr. Frederick Wertham, Psychiatrist, Director, LaFargue Clinic, New York, N.Y.," April 21, 1954. www.thecomicbooks.com/wertham.html.

3. Quoted in TheComicBooks.com, "Testimony of William M. Gaines, Publisher, Entertaining Comics Group, New York, N.Y.," April 21, 1954. www.thecomicbooks.com/gaines.html.

4. Surgeon General's Scientific Advisory Committee on Television and Social Behavior, *Television and Growing Up: The Impact of Televised Violence*, National Institute of Mental Health, 1972. http://profiles.nlm.nih.gov/NN/B/C/H/F/_/nnbchf.ocr.

Chapter 1

Is Media Violence a Problem?

Since the beginnings of television the effects of media violence on children has been a controversial subject.

Media Violence Has Harmful Effects on Young People

Bart Peterson

"By the time they turn 18, young people will witness 40,000 killings and 200,000 violent incidents."

In the following viewpoint Bart Peterson argues that young people today are bombarded with violent images through a variety of media: video games, television, and films. He claims that many scientific studies support the view that media violence is harmful to children. Peterson contends that more must be done to protect children from the harmful effects of media violence. He suggests several solutions, including more involvement on the part of parents and community leaders to hold retailers accountable and help young people avoid media violence. Peterson is the senior vice president of corporate affairs and communications for Eli Lilly and Company and the former Democratic mayor of Indianapolis, Indiana.

Bart Peterson, "Protecting Our Children from Harmful Media Violence," *Nation's Cities Weekly*, vol. 30, October 29, 2007, pp. 2, 12. Reproduced by permission.

AS YOU READ, CONSIDER THE FOLLOWING QUESTIONS:
 1. The average American youth spends how many hours per week exposed to media, according to Peterson?
 2. According to the author, more than three hundred scientific studies have shown a link between what two things?
 3. What two organizations does the author identify as providing guidance to parents on media violence?

Every day, in the virtual world of violent video games, young people witness—and even control—violent acts that take the lives of innocent victims—including children and police officers. Punching buttons on a controller connected to their favorite video game console, youthful players take aim with a variety of weapons at their disposal. Moving from target to target, images on the screen become more graphic and more violent. Young people viewing many of today's highest grossing films or top-rated television shows are similarly faced with gory, often gratuitous, violent acts.

A Culture of Violence

As a mayor, I am concerned about the impact that this "culture of violence" is having on our young people and our communities. As elected leaders of our communities, I believe we have a responsibility to call attention to this problem—to help educate our parents, businesses and others about these impacts and to begin conversations to raise their awareness.

The facts speak for themselves: the average American youth spends more than 45 hours per week exposed to all types of media—television, film, video games, the Internet and music. By the time they turn 18, young people will witness 40,000 killings and 200,000 violent incidents.

Experts from the U.S. Surgeon General's office, the National Institute of Mental Health, the American Academy of Pediatrics and the American Psychological Association have all concluded that repeated exposure to media violence can lead children to view violence as an acceptable means of settling conflicts, become emotionally desensitized to violence and be more likely to exhibit violent behavior themselves. Both the Federal Trade Commission and the Federal Communications Commission have weighed in on the impacts of media violence on children.

There is a common message coming from all these groups: More must be done to protect our children from the harmful effects of media violence.

The Scientific Studies

At a national summit on media violence hosted by NLC [National League of Cities] last spring [2007] in Indianapolis, we brought together noted scientific, academic and entertainment industry experts, as well as municipal officials and law enforcement to address the growing violence found in our popular culture and its effects on children.

Critics of media violence cite over three hundred studies that show a direct link between media violence, such as in video games, and aggressive behavior.

We learned that more than 300 scientific studies have shown a direct link between exposure to media violence and aggressive behavior. Certainly, media violence is only one of several risk factors that may lead to violent behavior. But we know that any type of violence, real or virtual, affects children.

"If a child is exposed to any behavior repeatedly, that's how they learn," said Jeff McIntyre of the American Psychological Association.

I am encouraged by the efforts of some members of Congress to address this issue while working to protect fundamental rights of free speech. But we don't have to wait for congressional action or more regulation to make a difference. Mayors, neighborhood leaders, teachers and others can start now and bring this important topic front and center in their own communities.

Protecting Young People

First and foremost, we must help our children navigate the minefield that is modern media and understand the world in which they live. We must pay attention to what our kids are watching and doing.

Anticipating the concern from parents who say they don't have time or aren't savvy enough, several organizations, including Common Sense Media and Pause Parent Play, have done the work for them, reviewing films, video games and television, and offering specific guidance and advice through their websites.

We also must be mindful that it is our responsibility when our kids see violence in films, on television and in video, to discuss with them what the consequences of that violence would be in a real world context—consequences to the victim's as well as the perpetrator's families and to the community at large.

As municipal leaders, we must be prepared to help stimulate dialogue with parent-teacher associations (PTAs), school district administrators and teachers, youth councils, civic and community

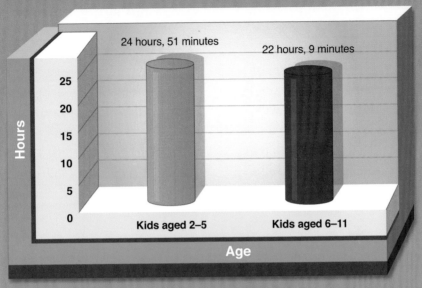

The Average Hours Kids Spend Watching Television per Week

24 hours, 51 minutes

22 hours, 9 minutes

Hours

25

20

15

10

5

0

Kids aged 2–5

Kids aged 6–11

Age

Taken from: Patricia McDonough, "TV Viewing Among Kids at an Eight-Year High," Nielson Company, October 26, 2009. http://blog.nielson.com/nielsenwire/media_entertainment/tv-viewing-among-kids-at-an-eight-year-high.

groups, advertisers and retailers. We must call upon the entertainment industry to show more of the consequences of violence and continue to hold our local retailers accountable as they voluntarily restrict sales of "Mature" and "R" rated media to young people. And we must also celebrate the positive choices made by so many of our young people today and continue to offer real options for them to counter the lure of hours spent in front of a television or computer screen.

NLC is working in partnership with the National PTA to provide resource materials to those of us in city leadership who want to take steps to start a discussion locally. This week [in October 2007], every NLC member city will receive a mailing that includes NLC's DVD on media violence, recommended steps for municipal leaders to consider, and a sample city resolution, as well as educational materials developed by the PTA. All of these materials will also be located online at the NLC website.

I urge you to use these resources and reach out to other leaders and families in your communities. Our leadership on this issue can make an important difference in protecting young people from the harmful effects of media violence—for the sake of our next generation, our communities and the future health and welfare of our society.

EVALUATING THE AUTHOR'S ARGUMENTS:

In this viewpoint Bart Peterson claims that media violence has harmful effects on young people. In what ways does the author of the following viewpoint, Karen Sternheimer, disagree with Peterson?

Media Should Not Be Blamed for Problems Among Young People

Karen Sternheimer

"Poverty and family abuses, not steamy TV and violent rap music, are the best predictors of violence, drug and alcohol abuse, and unplanned pregnancy among youths."

In the following viewpoint Karen Sternheimer argues that the media are incorrectly blamed for a host of teenage problems. Although researchers claim that teen violence, drug use, and poor academic achievement are the result of television, movies, video games, music, and Internet use, Sternheimer claims that the statistics do not back up this link. She notes that the small number of studies that show a link are inconclusive, and studies that deny such a link usually do not get published. Sternheimer is a sociologist at the University of Southern California and the author of *Kids These Days: Facts and Fictions About Today's Youth* and *It's Not the Media: The Truth About Pop Culture's Influence on Children.*

AS YOU READ, CONSIDER THE FOLLOWING QUESTIONS:
1. The author claims that a 2008 study declared violent Internet sites the most important factor in promoting what?
2. The author reports that according to the Federal Bureau of Investigation, teen murder dropped by what percentage from 1990 to 2007?
3. According to Sternheimer, how many teens out of sixteen hundred reported both visiting violent Web sites and committing a seriously violent act?

A barrage of studies now proclaims that a single source causes nearly all bad behaviors among young people: "the media." Researchers announce that teenagers' smoking, drinking, pregnancy, obesity, poor academic achievement, violence, and other troubles overwhelmingly derive from television, movies, video games, music, and Internet use.

Media and Youth

Studies announcing that new forms of media damage kids now claim previously feared influences are unimportant. A 2008 study declaring violent Internet sites the most important media factor promoting teen violence concluded that television, music, movies, and video games really aren't big deals. A new report branding sexy TV shows a major cause of teenage pregnancy also finds, contrary to previous beliefs, that viewing other TV shows predicts less pregnancy.

Old notions that cigarette ads incite teen smoking have yielded to newer studies blaming television viewing, or simply having a TV in the bedroom. Now, the latest study fingers smoking in movies as the pivotal instigator of teen smoking, downplaying television and other previously suspected influences.

Researchers disagree about what forms of media most corrupt youth, but they agree that "media are increasingly pervasive in the lives of children and adolescents" and "newer forms of media seem to be especially concerning." Indeed, just 15 years ago [1993], the types of media researchers now find so devastating didn't exist or were less graphic. Explicit rap music, ultra-violent first-person video games, Internet sites, increased smoking in movies, sexual explicitness in prime time, advertisements employing sophisticated suggestion, and brutally realistic movie mayhem intensified in the last decade and a half.

And this leads to a bizarre contradiction: The more objectionable media available to youth, the bigger the declines in their rates of violence, pregnancy, and other risky behaviors.

The Statistics

The FBI reports that from 1990 through 2007, rates of serious violent and property crime among youths under age 18 plunged by 49%, including unprecedented declines in murder (down 66%),

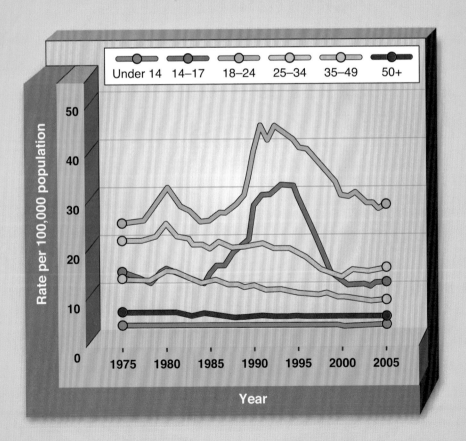

Acts of Homicide by Age, 1976–2005

Under 14   14–17   18–24   25–34   35–49   50+

Rate per 100,000 population

Year

rape (down 52%), robbery (down 32%), and serious assault (down 28%). The National Crime Victimization Survey finds even larger declines in teens' violent victimizations. The Centers for Disease Control reports massive declines in teenagers' rates of giving birth (down 30% since 1990), pregnancies (down 40%), gun deaths (down 55%), suicide (down 30%), and violent deaths (down 37%). Large-scale surveys such as Monitoring the Future and The American Freshman find students today reporting higher levels of happiness, optimism, leadership interest, and volunteerism and lower rates of smoking, drinking, depression, dropout, and materialism. Youngest teens show the biggest improvements.

How do we reconcile surveys claiming young people increasingly suffer from media-inflicted damage with solid statistics showing massive improvements in young people's real-life attitudes and behaviors? Decades of research warn that surveys and experiments are easily biased tools vulnerable to unreliable results. Subjects can be powerfully influenced to confirm the researchers' beliefs even when researchers conduct studies ethically. That's why researchers usually produce results consistent with what they and their funders already believe. In a notable example, respected media-violence scientists claimed *Sesame Street* and *Mr. Rogers' Neighborhood* provoked aggressive behaviors in children.

Recently, researchers reported that most published studies find the media are "crucial" contributors to "negative health results for children." The study, not incidentally, was funded by Common Sense Media, a lobbying group whose mission statement declares that "media and entertainment profoundly impact the social, emotional, and physical development of our nation's children." Its researchers produced favorable results by downplaying a key fact: journal editors and reviewers notoriously favor studies that find significant results and rarely publish studies that find no effects.

FAST FACT

According to the Office of Juvenile Justice and Delinquency Prevention, part of the U.S. Department of Justice, from 1997 to 2005 the juvenile delinquency caseload dropped by 9 percent.

Some critics of media violence have gone so far as to say that even seemingly innocuous shows like Sesame Street *provoke aggressive behavior in children.*

The Truth About Media Influence

A 2007 review in *Aggression and Violent Behavior* found that studies reporting negative effects from playing video games were far more likely to be published than equally good studies that didn't. Recognizing this problem, the *New England Journal of Medicine* is now seeking previously unpublished studies that failed to find significant effects. Even when published, studies that demonstrate no identifiable link between the media and problem youth behavior garner little media attention.

Even taken at face value, studies typically find only tiny percentages of teenagers are affected by media influences. For example, only a few dozen of the 1,500 teens surveyed in a widely publicized study watched the most sexually explicit TV shows and experienced a pregnancy. Just 30 of the 1,600 teens surveyed in another study reported both visiting violent websites and committing a seriously violent act. These tiny numbers—around 2% of the teens studied—form the basis of sweeping expert claims and alarming news headlines that

Internet sites, video games, and TV are instigating mass teenage misbehaviors.

Popular culture may often offend sensibilities, but in truth, it's not the central cause of social ills. It's time for science journal editors to implement more rigorous standards to rein in the flood of questionable survey studies whose sensational "findings" are diverting attention from truly significant problems. Poverty and family abuses, not steamy TV and violent rap music, are the best predictors of violence, drug and alcohol abuse, and unplanned pregnancy among youths.

Even as the recession and rising medical costs price health care out of reach for poorer and middle-class Americans, health researchers and medical journals publish more and more headline-grabbing "studies" blaming kids' media consumption for health crises.

President-elect Barack Obama's platform of change offers a tremendous opportunity for innovative health and crime policies focusing on real causes, rather than the easy politics of blaming teenagers and popular culture demons for the nation's social problems. "Turn off the TV," "put away the video games," and similar attacks on fictional entertainment images play well on the campaign stump, but real conditions like poverty, deficient health care, and family instability require our undivided attention if real change is the goal.

EVALUATING THE AUTHOR'S ARGUMENTS:

In this viewpoint Karen Sternheimer claims that the decrease in teen violence during the very same period that new violent media was on the rise proves that no link exists between the two. How do you think other authors in this chapter who claim a link between media violence and youth violence—namely Bart Peterson and Robert Peters—would explain this apparent contradiction?

Viewpoint

3

Media Violence Has Contributed to an Increase in Mass Murder

"The general consensus, supported by a mountain of anecdotal evidence and hundreds of social science research studies, is that entertainment violence does impact vulnerable youth in particular."

Robert Peters

In the following viewpoint Robert Peters claims that mass murder by individuals has increased in the United States. Peters denies that guns are to blame and believes that a decline in religious influence is part of the problem. Peters points to the change in popular culture as another main contributor to the increase in mass murder. He believes that the increased violence in film and television, along with the glamorization of gangsters and other criminals, contributes to the propensity for murder, especially in vulnerable young people. Peters is president of Morality in Media, an organization that works to combat pornography and to maintain standards of decency in the media.

AS YOU READ, CONSIDER THE FOLLOWING QUESTIONS:
1. According to Peters, what did articles in the news media call for after the mass murder school shooting at Virginia Tech?
2. The author claims that the film industry in the United States has changed in recent years by glamorizing and celebrating what?
3. According to Peters, the Federal Communications Commission issued a report in 2007 urging lawmakers to do what?

M ass murder by individuals who are not terrorists is not a new phenomenon. What is new in the United States is the regularity with which it now takes place. . . .

Guns and Religion

Following the horrific mass murder [of thirty-two people by one shooter] that occurred at Virginia Tech on April 16, 2007, the news media was filled with articles calling for more regulation of guns as the answer to that senseless crime and similar shootings.

Clearly, guns are the weapons of choice of mass murderers in the United States. Equally clear, assault weapons designed not to hunt game put rather to take human life have contributed to the increase in mayhem.

For these and other reasons, while I do recognize that the Second Amendment gives citizens a right to keep and bear arms, I also support government regulation of guns. Just as the liberty of speech and press is not an absolute right, neither is the right to keep and bear arms.

But should we place the primary blame for mass murders on guns and assume that more laws to regulate guns will solve the problem? I don't think so for a number of reasons. . . .

Over the years, I have . . . asked others and myself this question, "What has changed in the U.S. that can explain the increase in mass murder by individuals in recent decades?"

I begin my answer to this question by saying that a big part of what has changed is that there is far less religious influence today. Admittedly, the influence of religion in this country has not always been for the better. For example, some Americans used the Bible to justify slavery. But in my opinion, the good has far, far outweighed the bad; and part of the good that religion brought is a commandment, "You shall not commit murder."...

Mass Murder and Popular Culture

Another part of my answer to the question about what has changed in the United States is that the film industry now wallows in, glamorizes and celebrates murder, revenge, and sadism and depicts it as graphically as possible. Consider, for example, films like *Clockwork Orange, Straw Dogs, Reservoir Dogs, Texas Chain Saw Massacre, Natural Born Killers, Pulp Fiction, American Psycho, Saw, Hostel, Hills Have Eyes* and many others like them.

Guns are also the weapons of choice in Hollywood films and TV programs, with explosives not far behind. A week never goes by without at least one advertisement for a film that prominently depicts one or more individuals who are carrying, pointing or shooting one or more guns. Network promotions for TV programs also frequently depict guns.

Guns in the media, of course, are not a new phenomenon. In the 1950s and 1960s, guns were popular in both films and TV programs

"School Shooting," cartoon by Ed Fischer, www.CartoonStock.com.

that depicted war, the Wild West, police work and a wide variety of crimes, including organized crime.

And these films and TV programs did have an impact on us. For example, I still have a picture of my older brother and me with our cowboy six guns and holsters; and I still have memories of playing war in the woods with our toy rifles and my favorite gun, a plastic carbine!

But for the children of my generation it was clear who were the good guys and bad guys. Good guys took human life when they were justified in doing so. Bad guys committed murder.

I still remember watching the violent TV program *The Untouchables* (1959–1963) starring Robert Stack as FBI Agent Elliot Ness. I don't recall any classmate wanting to be a brutal gangster like Al Capone. We wanted to be the G-men [government men] who put gangsters away.

Compare the *Untouchables* treatment of gangsters with gangster portrayals in films made after Hollywood abandoned its Hays Code [Motion Picture Production Code] in 1968, like *Godfather, Scarface* and *Goodfellas*. And for many, TV's Tony Soprano will forever be their favorite "anti-hero."

The General Consensus

TV violence prompted Congress to hold hearings on three different occasions in the 1950s and again in the 1960s, 1970s and 1990s. In 2004, a bipartisan group of House members requested a report from the FCC [Federal Communications Commission] about TV violence. In 2007, the FCC issued its report urging lawmakers to restrict violent TV programming. In 2007, the Parents Television Council also issued a report, *Dying to Entertain: Violence on Broadcast Television, 1998–2006*, which concluded that TV violence "has become not only more frequent, but more graphic in recent years."

Violence in music and rap lyrics prompted Congress to hold hearings in 1985, 1997 and 2007. The marketing of violent films to children prompted Congress to hold hearings in 2000. Violence in videogames prompted Congress to hold hearings in 2006. The rash of shootings in schools prompted Congress to hold hearings in 1999 on "Youth Culture and Violence."

The general consensus, supported by a mountain of anecdotal evidence and hundreds of social science research studies, is that entertainment violence does impact vulnerable youth in particular. There are, of course, those who disagree with this consensus including businesses that profit from violent films, TV programs, rap lyrics and videogames.

In reporting on mass murders, the news media invariably discover that the perpetrator had problems at home, school or work or with a girlfriend or with people in general or had a history of emotional problems or mental illness. And these can be causative factors.

But there have always been people of all ages who had problems at home, school or work or with a girlfriend or with people in general

Many blame Hollywood's romanticization of gangster stereotypes such as Tony Montana in Scarface *for the rise in the murder rate.*

or who had a history of emotional problems or mental illness. Until recently, however, these problems didn't lead to regular mass murders!

The breakdown of the family can also be a factor, but mass murderers, including the Virginia Tech killer and both Columbine High School killers [who killed thirteen people in 1999], came from intact families.

Something else must be at work; and I would contend that what is at work is a popular culture that is in large measure nihilistic [resistant to laws and regulation] and hostile to religion, that prides itself in portraying anti-social behavior "non-judgmentally" and that wallows in and glamorizes murderous violence.

EVALUATING THE AUTHOR'S ARGUMENTS:

In this viewpoint Robert Peters claims that media violence has contributed to the increase in mass murder, particularly among youth. How would authors of contrasting viewpoints in this chapter—namely Karen Sternheimer and Ruth Conniff—dispute this claim? Is there a point of disagreement with Peters where these two authors agree?

Media Violence Leads to Callousness

Ruth Conniff

"For all of us— albeit some more than others— violent media change the way we think and feel."

In the following viewpoint Ruth Conniff argues that the emotional impact of media violence is significant. Although she does not advocate censorship, she is concerned particularly about the impact of media violence on young children. She claims that the impact of media violence on the young and the mentally ill is especially worrisome. Specifically, Conniff is concerned that violent media harm human sentiment, making people callous—indifferent to real human suffering. Conniff covers national politics for the *Progressive*, a monthly magazine committed to nonviolence and freedom of speech.

AS YOU READ, CONSIDER THE FOLLOWING QUESTIONS:

1. Conniff claims that adults, numbed by a large amount of violent media, are blind to what?
2. According to the author, the young and the mentally ill share what trait relevant to consumption of violent media?
3. Conniff claims that too much violence causes people to do what?

Ruth Conniff, "Contemplating Horror Is No Good for Us," *The Progressive,* April 24, 2007. Reproduced by permission of *The Progressive,* 409 East Main Street, Madison, WI 53703. www.progressive.org.

I was volunteering in my daughter's kindergarten classroom recently when I noticed one little girl sitting at the table silently, head down, with tears running down her cheeks. "What's wrong?" I asked her. "Scary movie," she whimpered. It was the second time this year, that I know of, that a five year old in my daughter's class has been so disturbed by something she saw on TV, it interfered with her ability to pay attention the next day in school. Who knows what awful images are haunting these children, for whom the line between fantasy and reality is still a blur?

The Emotional Impact of Violence

Adults, numbed by a barrage of violent images, seem blind to the emotional impact of shows like *CSI*, or even horror movies. "It's not real," they tell kids, impatient for them to grow callous to the contemplation of imaginary horrors.

As a scary movie wimp myself, I feel awful for these kids. I wish I could get inside their heads and erase those terrible scenes. Better yet, I wish I could do something to protect them in the first place, so that their natural empathy could be nurtured, not stomped on.

I'm treading on dangerous ground here, I know. It smacks of overbearing paternalism to talk about protecting kids from their own parents' choices of appropriate TV viewing. *The Progressive* is also a staunch First Amendment defender, reflexively supportive of the folks who condemned Tipper Gore [wife of former vice president Al Gore] for her music and video ratings crusade.

But we have to admit that something creepy is happening in our culture, when younger and younger children are spending more and more time marinating in a stew of violent, misogynist, and just generally anti-human images.

Fantasy and Reality

Don't get me wrong, I don't think that the shooting at Virginia Tech [in 2007 that left thirty-two dead] could have been averted if only we'd had a better ratings system for violent movies. Easy access to guns is a much bigger problem than kids seeing gun violence in movies. But it was striking that [the shooter] Cho Seung-Hui chose to take a video of himself in violent-action-movie poses and send it to NBC the day of the shootings. Fantasy and reality are blurry for the mentally ill, just like the very young. For all of us—albeit some more than others— violent media change the way we think and feel.

In a defiant act of callousness Virginia Tech shooter Cho Seung-Hui took a video of himself in violent-action-movie poses and sent it to NBC the day of the shootings.

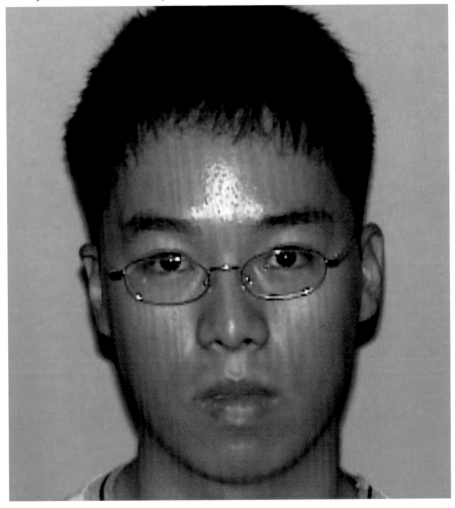

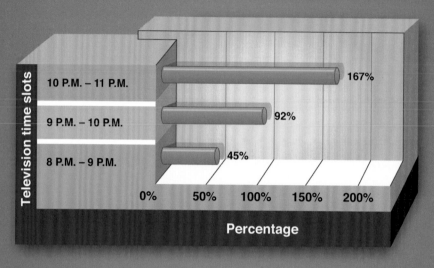

Increase in Broadcast Television Violence Between 1998 and 2006

Television time slots

- 10 P.M. – 11 P.M. — 167%
- 9 P.M. – 10 P.M. — 92%
- 8 P.M. – 9 P.M. — 45%

0% 50% 100% 150% 200%

Percentage

Taken from: Caroline Schulenburg, "Dying to Entertain: Violence on Prime Time Broadcast Television, 1998 to 2006," Parents Television Council, January 2007. www.parentstv.org/ptc/publications/reports/violencestudy/exsummary.asp.

Here's another example: Last Saturday night I went to see the [Los Angeles–based] Actor's Gang production of George Orwell's *1984*. Frankly, the play felt assaultive to me—two and a half hours of watching the main character be intermittently electrocuted while he recounted his story. Pretty gruesome stuff. In one of the last scenes, strapped into an electric chair, he is forced to endure higher and higher voltage shocks, then, in a realization of his worst nightmare, he is menaced by rats. Actually, I left right before the rat scene. I'd had enough. The play is considerably more unrelieved than Orwell's book, with special touches like flashlights shining in audience members' eyes and music played so loud it hurts your ears.

Standing outside the theater after the play, I saw a mother and young child—she looked about eight—coming out. The girl's face was pale and creased with distress. What on earth was her mother thinking?

Human Sentiment and Callousness

I know what [director] Tim Robbins and the Actors Gang are thinking: that shocking the audience will awaken its conscience.

Confronted by horror, we will be moved to take political action (in Orwell's time, against totalitarianism in the Soviet Union and fascism in Europe. In ours, against the government of George W. Bush). But I think the opposite is true. Bombarded by too much violence, we retreat and withdraw. Visceral revulsion overwhelms humane sentiment. We don't become more engaged or thoughtful when someone is beating us over the head.

The day after I saw *1984*, the *New York Times* ran a front-page story about torture of suspected insurgents by Iraqi troops. I flipped the paper over, not wanting to explain the blindfolded man in the accompanying photo to my three- and five-year-old daughters. Yes, we need to know about the real horrors committed or abetted by our government so we can help stop them. But raising our children to be callous to the idea of human suffering won't help.

EVALUATING THE AUTHOR'S ARGUMENTS:

In this viewpoint Ruth Conniff contends that media violence is not a direct cause of real-life violence. On this point she agrees with Karen Sternheimer, author of an earlier viewpoint, but in what key way does her view differ from the arguments of Sternheimer?

Chapter 2

Does Media Violence Lead to Real Violence?

The controversy over the effects of violent video games has raged for decades.

Viewpoint

1

Video Game Violence May Contribute to Copycat Violence

"We must determine if Moore and other murderers like him are anomalies or if ultra-violent video games dangerously warp the psyches of our youth."

Rebecca Hagelin

In the following viewpoint Rebecca Hagelin recounts a 2003 crime committed by a teenager who spent lots of time playing a violent video game. She points to similarities between the teenager's crime and the video game in order to support the view that playing violent video games may contribute to copycat violence by those who play the games. Hagelin claims that congressional hearings to explore the link between video game violence and copycat violence are necessary. Although she denies that the government is ultimately responsible for protecting children, she notes that society does protect minors from harmful materials in other arenas. Hagelin is the senior communications fellow at the Heritage Foundation, a conservative public policy research institute, and the author of *30 Ways in 30 Days to Save Your Family.*

1. According to Hagelin, in what ways was Devin Moore's crime like the video game *Grand Theft Auto*?
2. What is it about teenagers' brains, according to the author, that could increase the possibility of a link between video game violence and actual violence?
3. Hagelin believes that it is not the role of government but the role of whom to protect children from video games?

"Life is like a video game. Everyone has to die sometime."

If you spent part of your youth playing "Pac-Man" and "Space Invaders," such a statement must seem bizarre. Video games were . . . well, games—innocent diversions that did nothing worse than eat up dotted lines and too much of our allowances. A waste of time? Perhaps. But nobody got hurt.

At least, they didn't used to.

Copycat Violence

The opening statement above was spoken by Devin Moore, a teenager who murdered three people—two police officers and a 911 dispatcher—in a Fayettesville, Ala., police station in 2003. Arrested on suspicion of car theft, Moore was brought in for booking and ended up on a bloody rampage.

He lunged at Officer Arnold Strickland, grabbed his gun and shot him twice. Officer James Crump, who responded to the sound of the gunfire, was shot three times. And before he ran outside with police car keys he snatched, Moore put five bullets in Dispatcher Ace Mealer. Was this the first time Moore had committed such a heinous crime? Yes and no.

Moore was a huge fan of a notorious video game called *Grand Theft Auto*. As the title suggests, the goal is to steal cars. If that's all there was to the "game" it would be bad enough, but it gets worse: the way to acquire and hold on to the cars is to kill the police officers who try to stop you. And the sick minds behind the game give you plenty of choices—shooting them with a rifle, cutting them up with a chainsaw, setting them on fire, decapitation.

If you shoot an officer, you get extra points for shooting him in the head. It's no surprise, then, that all of Moore's real-life victims had their heads blown off.

According to court records, Moore spent hundreds of hours playing *Grand Theft*, which has been described as "a murder simulator."

But this time, his victims weren't a collection of animated pixels on a TV screen. They were flesh-and-blood human beings whose lives were snuffed out in seconds. They had families who continue to mourn their loss—such as Steve Strickland, Officer Strickland's brother. Tomorrow [March 28, 2006], he will testify before the U.S. Senate Judiciary Committee's Subcommittee on the Constitution, Civil Rights and Property. Chaired by Sen. Sam Brownback, R-Kan., the purpose of the hearing is to examine the constitutionality of state laws regulating the sale of ultra-violent video games to children. Three

Devin Moore killed three people in Alabama. He spent hundreds of hours playing the Grand Theft Auto *video game.*

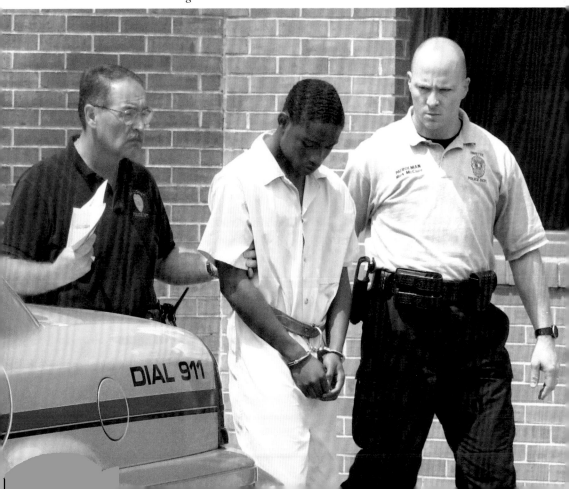

psychologists will testify about the potential link between playing violent video games and copycat violence, and whether the games contribute to aggressive behavior.

Video Games and Teens

With the ever-expanding use of technology by our children, such hearings are critical. We must determine if Moore and other murderers like him are anomalies or if ultra-violent video games dangerously warp the psyches of our youth. Those tempted to scoff at the connection between video games and behavior should bear a couple of things in mind. First, video games are not passive or spectator media. While playing the game, teenage boys and young men, the largest users of video games, actually *become* the characters who cut up their victims with chainsaws, set them on fire, or chop off their heads.

According to Dr. Elizabeth Carll of the American Psychological Association (who also will testify tomorrow), this active participation enhances the "learning" experience. And video games are often played repeatedly for hours on end—so, hour after hour, teens playing games such as *Grand Theft Auto* "learn" how to kill police officers and earn points for their barbarianism.

> **FAST FACT**
>
> According to *The Guinness World Records 2009 Gamer's Edition, Grand Theft Auto: San Andreas* was the most successful video game of the Playstation 2, with more than 17 million copies sold for that console, of a total of more than 21 million copies sold.

The second fact to keep in mind is that teenagers' brains are still developing and are extremely impressionable. The parents of teens hardly need reminding that for all their joys, teens often lack judgment, critical thinking skills, and foresight. Some are better than others, yes, but many (like Moore) are startlingly deficient. In short: Put a "murder simulator" in their hands, and you just might be asking for trouble. But don't put words in my mouth—I am not saying that every kid that plays a violent video game will become a criminal.

Arguments over Video Games

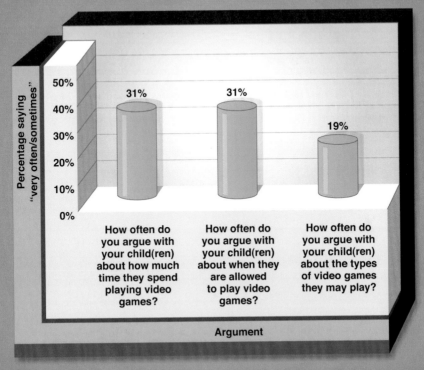

Note: Percentages may not add up to exactly 100 due to rounding.

Taken from: The Harris Poll #125, December 14, 2007.

The Role of Government

And as a staunch conservative who believes that "the government that governs least governs best," I'm not advocating a plethora of laws that may have a chilling effect on free speech. I do, however, recognize that it is sometimes necessary to provide special protections for minors from harmful materials—take pornography and alcohol, for example. As a mother, I also believe that our nation must examine how the products of our toxic culture affect the civility and safety of our children and of our society. We owe it to the students who died at Columbine [High School in 1999 in a shooting]; we owe it to Devin Moore's victims; we owe it to our own children.

But armed with the truth, and a God-given mandate to train our own children, we must never depend on government to take care of our kids or raise them. Parents must wake up to the fact that our nation's boys are being used and manipulated by an industry making billions of dollars by warping their minds. As I outline in my book, *Home Invasion: Protecting Your Family in a Culture That's Gone Stark Raving Mad*, it doesn't take an act of Congress to take back your home—it takes active, loving, informed parenting. It takes setting boundaries and sticking with them. It takes understanding our kids, and understanding that our kids need us to guide them. Senator Brownback is taking a bold step and doing his job as an elected official in exploring the effects of video game violence—it's up to parents to use the information to protect our sons and our society.

EVALUATING THE AUTHOR'S ARGUMENTS:

In this viewpoint Rebecca Hagelin suggests that playing violent video games may cause people to act out the violence in real life. How would Christopher Orlet, the author of the next viewpoint, respond to Hagelin's suggestion?

Viewpoint 2

Video Games Should Not Be Blamed for Acts of Real Violence

Christopher Orlet

"You don't become a psychopath by simply playing video games."

In the following viewpoint Christopher Orlet expresses outrage at a pending lawsuit filed against several software manufactures and retailers on behalf of the victims of a teenaged murderer. The fact that the murderer frequently played violent video games does not explain his psychopathic behavior, argues Orlet, and suggests that the civil lawsuit is driven by greed rather than principle. Orlet claims that the real roots of violent behavior are elsewhere and calls for society to address these factors rather than being sidetracked by a concern about video games that are in poor taste. Orlet is a journalist who has written for the *American Spectator*, the *American Thinker*, and the *Wall Street Journal*, among other publications.

When 16-year-old Devin Thompson [also known as Devin Moore] shot down two Alabama police officers and a dispatcher in cold blood in 2003, local journalists, teachers, and coffee-shop commentators began the usual round of soul searching. Some wanted to point the finger at the boy's negligent parents. Some wanted to blame a wayward society that had in so many ways failed the boy-killer. A few even wanted to blame the boy himself. But the victims' families had other ideas.

Strickland v. Sony

It turns out the real guilty party was a software manufacturer. Also complicit in the homicides were corporations like Wal-Mart and Sony. According to a civil suit filed on behalf of relatives of two of the deceased, Take Two Interactive Software's crime-action game *Grand Theft Auto* "trained and motivated" Devin Thompson to steal a car, and, once apprehended by Fayette police officers, snatch a service revolver from one of [the] cops and open fire, finally making off in a stolen police car. During the melee officers Arnold Strickland, James Crump, and dispatcher Leslie Mealer were killed. Apprehended a second time Thompson, according to the AP [Associated Press], told the cops that, "Life is a video game. You got to die sometimes."

The defendant's attorney Jack Thompson told *Tuscaloosa News*, "What has happened in Alabama is that four companies participated in the training of Devin . . . to kill three men." Wal-Mart and Gamestop are named in the suit because clerks sold the video games to the 16-year-old Thompson (the *Grand Theft Auto* series is rated M for mature audiences 17 and older). Sony is being sued because . . . well, because they manufacture PlayStation 2 and *Grand Theft Auto*, like

Popular Video Game Genres

Genre (examples)

Genre	Percentage
Racing (*NASCAR, Mario Kart, Burnout*)	74%
Puzzle (*Bejeweled, Tetris, Solitaire*)	72%
Sports (*Madden, FIFA, Tony Hawk*)	68%
Action (*Grand Theft Auto, Devil May Cry, Ratchet and Clank*)	67%
Adventure (*Legend of Zelda, Tomb Raider*)	66%
Rhythm (*Guitar Hero, Dance Dance Revolution, Lumines*)	61%
Strategy (*Civilization IV, StarCraft, Command and Conquer*)	59%
Simulation (*The Sims, Rollercoaster Tycoon, Ace Combat*)	49%
Fighting (*Tekken, Super Smash Bros. Mortal Kombat*)	49%
First-person shooters (*Halo, Counter-Strike, Half-life*)	47%
Role-playing (*Final Fantasy, Blue Dragon, Knights of the Old Republic*)	36%
Survival horror (*Resident Evil, Silent Hill, Condemned*)	32%
Massively multiplayer online games (*World of Warcraft*)	21%
Virtual worlds (*Second Life, Gaia, Habbo Hotel*)	10%

0%   20%   40%   60%   80%   100%

Percentage of teens who report playing games in this genre

Taken from: Pew Internet & American Life Project, "Gaming and Civic Engagement Survey of Teens/Parents," November 2007–February 2008.

thousands of other video games, is designed to play on PlayStation 2. One wonders why the plaintiffs are not suing the manufacturers of the television set as well? [The lawsuit is still pending.]

Occasionally there is a single root cause for murder. These are called crimes of passion. But more often violent crimes are committed by young men with long histories of trouble and chaos. An

Devin Moore's attorney, Jack Thompson (pictured), blamed the manufacturers of Grand Theft Auto *for "training Devin . . . to kill 3 men."*

intelligent judge knows that it is often a multiplicity of factors that creates a psychopath: abuse, neglect, hopelessness, ignorance, laziness, absentee parents, and the plain, simple thrill of bad behavior. "Media violence," writes Craig A. Anderson, a media violence expert and chair of the department of psychology at Iowa State University, "is only one of many factors that contribute to societal violence, and is certainly not the most important one." However, for the trial lawyers and plaintiffs there is little benefit to be had in blaming hopelessness and ignorance (though I suppose one might sue the school district). Someone must be held accountable, preferably someone with deep pockets. Jack Thompson and his clients are seeking $600 million.

This is a fairly typical case for the Miami lawyer, whose mission is, in his words, "to hold accountable the entertainment industry for the harm it does to our children." Jack Thompson is perhaps best known for working on anti-obscenity crusades like his partnership with [actor and then-president of the National Rifle Association] Charlton Heston to persuade Time Warner to pull the song "Cop Killer" from Ice T's 1992 *Bodycount* LP, and bringing obscenity charges against the seminal rap band 2 Live Crew, which ultimately forced record companies to place warning labels on raunchy and misogynistic albums. However, in this instance the lawyer seems to be in it more for the cash than for any sense of justice. Asked about the suit by video game columnist Shaun McCormick, Thompson's response was a terse "Kiss the game industry good-bye."

The Real Causes of Violence
Only a moral zombie would defend asinine crime-action games ("murder simulators" to use the lawyer's parlance) like *Grand Theft Auto*, which appeals to the same sort of mindset that enjoys cockfighting and bear-baiting. Jack Thompson's one-stop-lawsuit website

offers this description of *Grand Theft Auto*: "In this game you have sex with a prostitute and then kill her grotesquely to get your money back and win the game faster. Police officers are set on fire, shotgunned in the face, and innocent pedestrians are run over with cars."

A kind of *Death Car 2000* without the satire. Besides the evidence is quite clear, as Prof. Anderson notes, that "high levels of violent video game exposure have been linked to delinquency, fighting at school and during free play periods, and violent criminal behavior. . . . It decreases the normal negative emotional reactions to conflict, aggression, and violence." But the same might be said for watching classic, though violent films like *Reservoir Dogs* and *Goodfellas.* That's why they are rated for mature audiences. The solution is not to ban games like *Grand Theft Auto*, as California Assembly woman Leland Yee has proposed. The solution is to address the real factors that create psychopathic boys. The solution, as [writer Henry David] Thoreau said, is to hack at the roots of evil, not prune the branches.

The Wal-Mart and Gamestop clerks were wrong to sell the mature-audiences-only game to a minor, and deserve to be fined and fired (not sued) for that, just as they would be ticketed for selling tobacco to a minor. Wal-Mart has largely stopped selling CDs and DVDs containing obscene lyrics, and it should likewise rethink its policy on selling games that portray criminal behavior as good times. It might also make sense to raise the age for mature video games to 18. But none of this would have saved the lives of officers Strickland and Crump and dispatcher Mealer. Devin Thompson never said the "game made me do it." He did, however, say that "the reason I shot those officers is I didn't want to go to jail." That's a psychopath talking. And you don't become a psychopath by simply playing video games.

EVALUATING THE AUTHOR'S ARGUMENTS:

In this viewpoint Christopher Orlet claims that it might make sense to raise the age for mature video games to eighteen. Would Rebecca Hagelin, the author of the previous viewpoint, likely agree with him? Why or why not?

There Is Evidence That Violent Video Games Increase Aggression

"Three kinds of research link violent video games to increased aggression."

Amanda Schaffer

In the following viewpoint Amanda Schaffer argues that scientific research supports a link between violent video games and aggression. She cites three different kinds of research supporting such a link. Although Schaffer admits there are flaws with each, she contends that overall the research supports what she believes is an intuitive link. Schaffer cautions that not all video games cause negative effects and, in fact, some video games can be used for very positive effects. Schaffer is a science and medical columnist for *Slate* and *Double X* magazines and a frequent contributor to the *New York Times* science section.

AS YOU READ, CONSIDER THE FOLLOWING QUESTIONS:

1. The author claims that video games have a potent impact on what?

2. Schaffer contends that becoming desensitized to gory images by playing violent video games could do what?
3. The author cites the use of video games as positive when used as a desensitization tool to treat what three conditions?

On *The Daily Show* on Thursday, April 26, [2007,] [host] Jon Stewart made short work of the suggestion that the Virginia Tech shooter, Cho Seung-Hui, might have been influenced by violent video games. (Cho may or may not have played the popular first-person-shooter game *Counter-Strike* in high school.) A potential video-game connection has also been dangled after past killings, to the irritation of bloggers. The reports are that shooter Lee Boyd Malvo played the game *Halo* before his sniper attacks around Washington, D.C., and that Columbine killers Eric Harris and Dylan Klebold loved *Doom*. Does the link between video games and violence hold up?

The Research About Violent Video Games

Pathological acts of course have multiple, complex causes and are terribly hard to predict. And clearly, millions of people play *Counter-Strike, Halo,* and *Doom* and never commit crimes. But the subtler question is whether exposure to video-game violence is one risk factor for increased aggression: Is it associated with shifts in attitudes or responses that may predispose kids to act out? A large body of evidence suggests that this may be so. The studies have their shortcomings, but taken as a whole, they demonstrate that video games have a potent impact on behavior and learning. Sorry, Jon Stewart, but you needn't be a fuddy-duddy to worry about the virtual worlds your child lives in.

Three kinds of research link violent video games to increased aggression. First, there are studies that look for correlations between exposure to these games and real-world aggression. This work suggests that kids who are more immersed in violent video games may be more likely to get into physical fights, argue with teachers, or display anger and hostility. Second, there is longitudinal research (measuring behavior over time) that assesses gaming habits and belligerence in a group of children. One example: A study of 430 third-, fourth-, and fifth-graders, published this year [2007] by psychologists Craig Anderson, Douglas Gentile, and Katherine Buckley, found that the kids who played more violent video games "changed over the school year to become more verbally aggressive, more physically aggressive," and less helpful to others.

Finally, experimental studies randomly assign subjects to play a violent or a nonviolent game, and then compare their levels of aggression. In work published in 2000, Anderson and Karen Dill randomly assigned 210 undergraduates to play *Wolfenstein 3-D*, a first-person-shooter game, or *Myst*, an adventure game in which players explore mazes and puzzles. Anderson and Dill found that when the students went on to play a second game, the *Wolfenstein 3-D* players were more likely to behave aggressively toward losing opponents. Given the chance to punish with blasts of noise, they chose to inflict significantly louder and longer blasts than the *Myst* kids did. Other recent work randomly assigned students to play violent or nonviolent games, and then analyzed differences in brain activation patterns using fMRI [functional magnetic resonance imaging] scans, but the research is so far difficult to assess.

Does Media Violence Lead to Real Violence?   49

An Intuitive Connection

Each of these approaches has its flaws. The first kind of correlational study can never prove that video-game playing *causes* physical aggression. Maybe aggressive people are simply more apt to play violent games in the first place. Meanwhile, the randomized trials, like Anderson and Dill's, which do imply causation, necessarily depend on lab-based measures of aggression, such as whether subjects blast each other with noise. This is a respected measure, but obviously not the same as seeing whether real people hit or shoot each other. The longitudinal work, like this year's elementary-school study, is a useful middle ground: It shows that across the board, playing more-violent video games predicts higher levels of verbal and physical aggression later on. It doesn't matter why the kids started playing violent games or whether they were already more aggressive than their peers; the point is that a year of game-playing likely contributes to making them more aggressive than they were when they started. If we had only one of the three kinds of studies, the findings wouldn't mean much. But taken together, the body of research suggests a real connection.

The connection between violent games and real violence is also fairly intuitive. In playing the games, kids are likely to become desensitized to gory images, which could make them less disturbing and perhaps easier to deal with in real life. The games may also encourage kids (and adults) to rehearse aggressive solutions to conflict, meaning that these thought processes may become more available to them when real-life conflicts arise, Anderson says. Video games also offer immediate feedback and constant small rewards—in the form of points, or access to new levels or weapons. And they tend to tailor tasks to a player's skill level, starting easy and getting harder. That makes them "phenomenal teachers," says Anderson, though "what they teach very much depends on content."

A study published in 2007 found that children who played violent video games became more verbally and physically aggressive and less helpful.

The Positive Aspects of Video Games

Critics counter that some kids may "use games to vent anger or distract themselves from problems," as psychiatry professor Cheryl Olson writes. This can be "functional" rather than unhealthy, depending on the kid's mental state and the extent of his game playing. But other studies suggest that venting anger doesn't reduce later aggressive behavior, so this thesis doesn't have the most solid support.

When video games aren't about violence, their capacity to teach can be a good thing. For patients suffering from arachnophobia [fear of spiders], fear of flying, or post-traumatic stress disorder, therapists are beginning to use virtual realities as a desensitization tool. And despite the rap that they're a waste of time, video games may also teach visual attention and spatial skills. (Recently, a study showed that having played three or more hours of video games a week was a better predictor of a laparoscopic surgeon's skills than his or her level of surgical training.) The games also work for conveying information to kids that they will remember. Video games that teach diabetic kids how to take better care of themselves, for instance, were shown to decrease their diabetes-related urgent and emergency visits by 77 percent after six months.

Given all of this, it makes sense to be specific about which games may be linked to harmful effects and which to neutral or good ones. Better research is also needed to understand whether some kids are more vulnerable to video-game violence, and how exposure interacts with other risk factors for aggression like poverty, psychological disorders, and a history of abuse. Meanwhile, how about a game in which kids, shrinks, and late-night comics size up all these factors and help save the world?

EVALUATING THE AUTHOR'S ARGUMENTS:

In this viewpoint Amanda Schaffer contends that the link between violent games and real violence is supported by science. Name at least one scientific study that the author of the next viewpoint—Daniel Koffler—cites in direct opposition to such a link.

There Is No Evidence That Violent Video Games Increase Aggression

Daniel Koffler

"There is no shortage of readily available literature on the relationship between media exposure and behavior, and the evidence does not support the prohibitionists' case."

In the following viewpoint Daniel Koffler argues that the recent attempts to ban the sale of violent and sexually explicit video games to minors are based on politics rather than on evidence. Koffler believes that politicians go after video games because of the lack of people willing to defend them. There is no evidence for the link between violent video games and aggression, claims Koffler, and he points to several studies that undermine the claim of such a link. As far as regulations go, Koffler argues that any regulation of video games is likely futile given the easy access to a wide variety of media choices. Koffler is a Clarendon Scholar and graduate student in philosophy at the University of Oxford.

Daniel Koffler, "Grand Theft Scapegoat," *Reason,* vol. 37, October 2005, p. 72-73. Copyright © 2005 by Reason Foundation, 3415 S. Sepulveda Blvd., Suite 400, Los Angeles, CA 90034, www.reason.com. Reproduced by permission.

AS YOU READ, CONSIDER THE FOLLOWING QUESTIONS:

1. The author claims that usually the strongest argument made in favor of video games is that they are what?
2. Koffler claims that the sales of video games grew by what amount between 1995 and 2003?
3. According to the author, what percentage of games is rated "Mature"?

I n May [2005], by a vote of 106 to 6, the Illinois legislature passed a measure banning the sale of "violent" and "sexually explicit" video games to minors [determined to be unconstitutional in 2006]. The California Assembly is considering its own version of a prohibition on game sales to the under-aged, and Washington, Indiana, and Missouri already have enacted similar laws, only to see them struck down on First Amendment grounds.

Targeting Video Games

Video games are an appealing target for a public figure in search of a crusade. Movies and music have energetic advocates, but it's hard to find anyone who will defend games for their artistic value, or even on the grounds of freedom of expression. Usually the strongest argument made for games is that they are harmless fun. That's not the most effective response when the governor of Illinois is claiming "too many of the video games marketed to our children teach them all of the wrong lessons and all of the wrong values."

Ominously, the Illinois proposal pays no heed to the existing range of voluntary content ratings, which run from EC ("Early Childhood") to AO ("Adults Only") and ostensibly allow game merchants to decide for themselves what constitutes "violent" or "sexually explicit" material. In a message "to the parents of Illinois," Democratic Gov. Rod Blagojevich asserts that "ninety-eight percent of the games considered suitable by the industry for teenagers contain graphic violence." Blagojevich is surely abusing language and statistics—if you stretch the phrase far enough, even the mild-mannered *Super Mario Bros.* includes what could be described as "graphic violence"—but the implication is that the proposed legislation's content restrictions could apply to games the ratings board approved for teens.

A Lack of Evidence

It would not be fair to say that the arguments for video game criminalization are completely uncontaminated by evidence. But prohibitionists are highly selective about the evidence they present and are careless once they've presented it, hoping to substitute raw emotional appeal for a plausible explanatory framework. Blagojevich, for example, claims "experts have found that exposure to violent video games increases aggressive thoughts, feelings, and behaviors"—as if no

Rockstar, the manufacturers of Grand Theft Auto: San Andreas, *were forced to reissue the game without hidden sexual content after Senator Hillary Clinton and others pressured the Federal Trade Commission to investigate the company.*

The Entertainment Software Rating Board's Content Symbols

Symbol	Description
EARLY CHILDHOOD / eC / CONTENT RATED BY ESRB	**Early Childhood** Titles rated EC (Early Childhood) have content that may be suitable for ages 3 and older. Contains no material that parents would find inappropriate.
EVERYONE / E / CONTENT RATED BY ESRB	**Everyone** Titles rated E (Everyone) have content that may be suitable for ages 6 and older. Titles in this category may contain minimal cartoon, fantasy, or mild violence and/or infrequent use of mild language.
EVERYONE 10+ / E 10+ / CONTENT RATED BY ESRB	**Everyone 10+** Titles rated E10+ (Everyone 10 and older) have content that may be suitable for ages 10 and older. Titles in this category may contain more cartoon, fantasy, or mild violence; mild language; and/or minimal suggestive themes.
TEEN / T / CONTENT RATED BY ESRB	**Teen** Titles rated T (Teen) have content that may be suitable for ages 13 and older. Titles in this category may contain violence, suggestive themes, crude humor, minimal blood, simulated gambling, and/or infrequent use of strong language.
MATURE 17+ / M / CONTENT RATED BY ESRB	**Mature** Titles rated M (Mature) have content that may be suitable for ages 17 and older. Titles in this category may contain intense violence, blood and gore, sexual content, and/or strong language.
ADULTS ONLY 18+ / AO / CONTENT RATED BY ESRB	**Adults Only** Titles rated AO (Adults Only) have content that should only be played by persons 18 years and older. Titles in this category may include prolonged scenes of intense violence and/or graphic sexual content and nudity.
RATING PENDING / RP / CONTENT RATED BY ESRB	**Rating Pending** Titles listed as RP (Rating Pending) have been submitted to the ESRB and are awaiting final rating. (This symbol appears only in advertising prior to a game's release).

Taken from: Entertainment Software Rating Board, "ESRB Rating Symbols." www.esrb.org.

more need be said about the causal relationship between playing video games and engaging in anti-social behavior. Such rhetoric implies that video game players are empty, infinitely corruptible ciphers.

There is no shortage of readily available literature on the relationship between media exposure and behavior, and the evidence does not support the prohibitionists' case. A 2004 study of "Short-Term Psychological and Cardiovascular Effects on Habitual Players," conducted by researchers at the University of Bologna, concluded that "owning videogames does not in fact seem to have negative effects on aggressive human behavior." A 2004 report in *The Journal of the American Medical Association* noted: "If video games do increase violent tendencies outside the laboratory, the explosion of gaming over the past decade from $3.2 billion in sales in 1995 to $7 billion in 2003, according to industry figures, would suggest a parallel trend in youth violence. Instead, youth violence has been decreasing."

Likewise, criminologist Joanne Savage contends in a 2004 issue of *Aggression and Violent Behavior* that "there is little evidence in favor of focusing on media violence as a means of remedying our violent crime problem." In the absence of a wave of real-life, game-inspired carnage, Harvard Medical School psychiatry professor Cheryl Olson, writing in the journal *Academic Psychiatry* in the summer of 2004, advised that "it's time to move beyond blanket condemnations and frightening anecdotes and focus on developing targeted educational and policy interventions based on solid data."

The Politics of Popular Culture

Unfortunately, blanket condemnations and frightening anecdotes are likely to be with us as long as they prove electorally profitable. In March [2005], Sens. Hillary Clinton (D-N.Y.), Joseph Lieberman (D-Conn.), Sam Brownback (R-Kan.), and Rick Santorum (R-Pa.) jointly proposed a $90 million appropriation to study the effects of games and other media on children. Apparently, no one on any of the senators' staffs could be bothered to point out that there already *is* plenty of credible research on precisely that question. Either that, or a bipartisan coalition of presidential aspirants calculated that bashing game designers could be a cheap way to endear themselves to family-values voters.

This is hardly the first time politicians have attempted to bludgeon popular culture into submission. (Recall the political grandstanding that followed past moral panics over movies, comic books, and rock music.) What separates efforts to curb children's exposure to video games from older, parallel campaigns is how profoundly out of touch they are with the realities of the entertainment choices available to children.

For example, Hillary Clinton—fresh from her collaboration with Santorum and Brownback, and consistent with her advertised principle of "fighting the culture of sex and violence in the media"—decided in mid-July to intervene in the controversy over the "Hot Coffee" mod for the game *Grand Theft Auto [GTA]: San Andreas*. Hot Coffee is a hidden component of the game's coding that, if unlocked via a program that can be freely downloaded from the Internet, will treat a player to scenes of grainy, polygonal sex. Outraged, Clinton wrote a letter to the Federal Trade Commission urging it to investigate whether Rockstar (the company that produces *GTA*) created the Hot Coffee content. She seemed oblivious to one of the first lessons a new Web surfer learns: There is a universe of free Internet pornography that anyone looking online for explicit sex can see without bothering to download and install a video game modification.

> **FAST FACT**
>
> In *Entertainment Software Association v. Blagojevich*, the Seventh Circuit Court of Appeals found a ban on video games with violent content unconstitutional and voided the requirement that games carry an "18" label.

Media Choices

The sheer scope of media choices renders futile any effort to rein in content through regulations. Occasional pixelated displays of violence and sex can be found in some games that are sometimes sold to children. (Sixteen percent of games are rated "Mature," and 16 percent of game buyers are under 18, according to the Entertainment Software Association.) These comprise a tiny part of the total array of media content freely available to anyone.

Legislators nevertheless are drafting self-righteous bills that practically beg to be overturned in court. With any luck, that will keep the prohibitionists occupied until they discover the next dire threat to our children.

EVALUATING THE AUTHOR'S ARGUMENTS:

In this viewpoint Daniel Koffler claims that evidence does not support the banning of video games. Explain one study cited by the author of the previous viewpoint, Amanda Schaffer, that contradicts Koffler.

Television Violence Increases Aggression in Children

Dale Kunkel

"*As exposure accrues over time, year in and year out, a child who is a heavy viewer of media violence is significantly more likely to behave aggressively.*"

In the following viewpoint Dale Kunkel argues that exposure to media violence poses a public health risk to children. He identifies three harmful effects of television violence, noting that one is at the core of the concern for public health. Kunkel claims that television violence is widespread and that the risk of harmful effects is increased because of the way such violence is sanitized and glamorized. He contends that such media violence is not a passing trend but has been stable over time. In conclusion, Kunkel calls for a public-policy response to media violence to address what he believes is the most pervasive factor contributing to real-world violence and aggression. Kunkel is a professor of communication at the University of Arizona and was the coprincipal investigator of the National Television Violence Study from 1994 to 1998.

Dale Kunkel, "Testimony: The Effects of Television Violence on Children," Hearing before the U.S. Senate Committee on Commerce, Science, and Transportation on the Impact of Media Violence on Children, June 26, 2007. Reproduced by permission of the author.

AS YOU READ, CONSIDER THE FOLLOWING QUESTIONS:

1. Which of the three categories of harmful effects from television violence does the author claim is at the core of the public health concern?
2. According to Kunkel, what percentage of television programs was found to contain violent material by the National Television Violence Study?
3. What statistic does the author cite to support his view that exposure to media violence is the most pervasive factor contributing to real-world violence and aggression?

C oncern on the part of the public and Congress about the harmful influence of media violence on children dates back to the 1950s and 1960s, and remains strong today. The legitimacy of that concern is corroborated by extensive scientific research that has accumulated over the past 40 years. Indeed, in reviewing the totality of empirical evidence regarding the impact of media violence, the conclusion that exposure to violent portrayals poses a risk of harmful effects on children has been reached by the U.S. Surgeon General, the National Institute of Mental Health, the National Academy of Sciences, the American Medical Association, the American Psychological Association, the American Academy of Pediatrics, and a host of other scientific and public health agencies and organizations.

The Harmful Effects on Children

These harmful effects are grouped into three primary categories: (1) children's learning of aggressive attitudes and behaviors; (2) desensitization, or an increased callousness towards victims of violence; and (3) increased or exaggerated fear of being victimized by violence. While all of these effects reflect adverse outcomes, it is the first—an increased propensity for violent behavior—that is at the core of public health concern about televised violence. The statistical relationship between children's exposure to violent portrayals and their subsequent aggressive behavior has been shown to be stronger than the relationship between asbestos exposure and the risk of laryngeal cancer; the relationship between condom use and the risk of contracting HIV; and exposure to second-hand smoke in the workplace and the risk of lung cancer. There is no controversy in the medical, public health, and social science communities about the risk of harmful effects from children's exposure to media violence. Rather, there is strong consensus that exposure to media violence is a significant public health concern.

Drawing upon evidence from the National Television Violence Study, as well as other related research, there are several evidence-based conclusions that can be drawn regarding the presentation of violence on television.

Widespread Sanitized and Glamorized Violence

Violence is widespread across the television landscape. Turn on a television set and pick a channel at random; the odds are better than 50-50 that the program you encounter will contain violent material. To be more precise, 60% of approximately 10,000 programs sampled for the National Television Violence Study contained violent material. That study identified an average of 6,000 violent interactions in a single week of programming across the 23 channels that were examined, including both broadcast and cable networks. More than half of the violent shows (53%) contained lethal acts, and one in four of the programs with violence (25%) depicted the use of a gun.

Most violence on television is presented in a manner that increases its risk of harmful effects on child-viewers. More specifically, most violence on television follows a highly formulaic pattern that is both sanitized and glamorized.

By sanitized, I mean that portrayals fail to show realistic harm to victims, both from a short and long-term perspective. Immediate pain and suffering by victims of violence is included in less than half of all scenes of violence. More than a third of violent interactions depict unrealistically mild harm to victims, grossly understating the severity of injury that would occur from such actions in the real world. In sum, most depictions sanitize violence by making it appear to be much less painful and less harmful than it really is.

By glamorized, I mean that violence is performed by attractive role models who are often justified for acting aggressively and who suffer

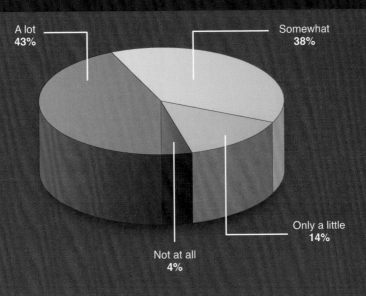

Parents' Views on Media Violence

How much, if at all, do you think exposure to violence in the media contributes to violent behavior in children?

A lot
43%

Somewhat
38%

Only a little
14%

Not at all
4%

Taken from: Kaiser Family Foundation, "Parents, Children, and Media," June 2007. www.kff.org.

no remorse, criticism, or penalty for their violent behavior. More than a third of all violence is committed by attractive characters, and more than two-thirds of the violence they commit occurs without any signs of punishment.

Violence that is presented as sanitized or glamorized poses a much greater risk of adverse effects on children than violence that is presented with negative outcomes such as pain and suffering for its victims or negative consequences for its perpetrators.

The Consistency of Television Violence

The overall presentation of violence on television has remained remarkably stable over time. The National Television Violence Study examined programming for three years in the 1990s and found a tremendous

Critics argue that television violence has been glamorized and sanitized to the point that viewers become desensitized to it.

degree of consistency in the pattern of violent portrayals throughout the television landscape. Across the entire study of roughly 10,000 programs, the content measures which examined the nature and extent of violence varied no more than a percent or two from year to year. Similar studies that have been conducted since that time have produced quite comparable results.

This consistency clearly implies that the portrayal of violence on television is highly stable and formulaic—and unfortunately, this formula of presenting violence as glamorized and sanitized is one that enhances its risk of harmful effects for the child audience.

In sum, the evidence clearly establishes that the level of violence on television poses substantial cause for concern. It demonstrates that violence is a central aspect of television programming that enjoys remarkable consistency and stability over time.

The Implications for Public Policy

It is well established by a compelling body of scientific evidence that television violence poses a risk of harmful effects for child-viewers. While exposure to media violence is not necessarily the most potent factor contributing to real world violence and aggression in the United States today, it is certainly the most pervasive. Millions of children spend an average of 20 or more hours per week watching television, and this cumulative exposure to violent images can shape young minds in unhealthy ways.

Given the free-speech guarantees of the First Amendment, the courts have ruled that there must be evidence of a "compelling governmental interest" in order for Congress to take action that would regulate television content in any way, such as the indecency regulations enforced by the FCC [Federal Communications Commission]. In my view, the empirical evidence documenting the risk of harmful effects from children's exposure to televised violence clearly meets this threshold, and I should note that former Attorney General Janet Reno offered an identical opinion to this Committee when she testified before it on this same issue in the 1990s. . . .

> **FAST FACT**
>
> According to a 2005 study by Kevin D. Browne and Catherine Hamilton-Giachritsis, an average of twenty to twenty-five violent acts are shown in children's television programs each hour in the United States.

It is the cumulative nature of children's exposure to thousands and thousands of violent images over time that constitutes the risk of harmful effects. Just as medical researchers cannot quantify the effect of smoking one cigarette, media violence researchers cannot specify the effect of watching just a single violent program. But as exposure accrues over time, year in and year out, a child who is a heavy viewer of media violence is significantly more likely to behave aggressively.

This relationship is the same as that faced by the smoker who lights up hour after hour, day after day, over a number of years, increasing their risk of cancer with every puff. . . .

To conclude, the research evidence in this area establishes clearly that the level of violence on television poses substantial cause for concern. Content analysis studies demonstrate that violence is a central aspect of television programming that enjoys remarkable consistency and stability over time. And effects research, including correlational, experimental, and longitudinal designs, converge to document the risk of harmful psychological effects on child-viewers. Collectively, these findings from the scientific community make clear that television violence is a troubling problem for our society.

EVALUATING THE AUTHOR'S ARGUMENTS:

In this viewpoint Dale Kunkel contends that the relationship between media violence and aggressive behavior is the same as the relationship between smoking and lung cancer. What objection would Jonathan L. Freedman, in the following viewpoint, have to this assertion?

There Is No Evidence That Television Violence Increases Aggression in Children

Jonathan L. Freedman

"The evidence is not overwhelming— indeed, it provides no good reason to believe that television violence causes aggression much less serious violence."

In the following viewpoint Jonathan L. Freedman argues that there is no evidence for the view that television violence causes aggression or violent crime. Freedman takes issue with a comparison made between the effects of media violence and the effects of smoking. He argues that the effects of media violence are not like the effects of smoking and explains what he believes would need to be shown in order to prove a connection between media violence and actual violence. Freedman also cites the crime rate over the last few decades in defense of the view that media violence does not cause aggression. Freedman is a professor of psychology at the University of Toronto and is the author of *Media Violence and Its Effect on Aggression: Assessing the Scientific Evidence*.

AS YOU READ, CONSIDER THE FOLLOWING QUESTIONS:
1. Freedman argues that there is no comparison between the effect of television violence on aggression and what other cause-and-effect correlation?
2. Freedman contends that a person who smokes regularly for twenty years is how much more likely to get lung cancer than someone who does not smoke?
3. According to Freedman, a sharp decline in violent crime in the United States started in what year?

The recent release [in April 25, 2007,] of the Federal Communications Commission (FCC) report on violent television programming and its call for restricting children's access to such programming has once more brought this issue to public attention. There have been many statements about this issue by psychologists, politicians, and others.

The Evidence

By those who believe that television violence is harmful, we have been told that there is overwhelming evidence that exposure to violence on television causes aggression (what I will call the causal hypothesis for convenience), that there is no longer any legitimate debate about this, and that the effect is as strong as the effect of cigarette smoking on cancer. We have even been told that the press is biased because it gives more time to the opposing view than is warranted—that since there is no question, the press should not even mention the other view.

None of this is correct. The evidence is not overwhelming—indeed, it provides no good reason to believe that television violence causes aggression much less serious violence. The debate is certainly not over although some would like it to be. There is no comparison between the effect of smoking on cancer and the effect of television violence on aggression. And the press has, if anything, given far too much attention to the causal hypothesis than to those who disagree with it. The most ardent advocates of the causal hypothesis seem to object to any disagreement or criticism of their position. However, their position is wrong, it deserves to be criticized, and it is time once more to set the record straight. . . .

Television Violence and Smoking

One of the most deceptive statements coming from those who favor the causal hypothesis is that the effect of television violence on aggression is as strong as the effect of smoking on lung cancer. This is hyperbole of the most egregious kind because it is not only wrong but might cause people to question the harmful effects of smoking. I am not an expert on the effects of smoking, but let me cite one figure: Someone who smokes regularly for 20 years is 10 to 20 times more likely to get lung cancer than someone who does not smoke.

There is nothing remotely comparable in any of the research on television violence. It is not true that someone who watches television violence for any length of time, no matter how long, is many times more likely to commit a violent crime than someone who does not watch. In fact, there is no reliable evidence that television violence causes any violent crimes. And even with minor aggression, there is no evidence that watching violent television causes people to be many times more likely to be aggressive. It does not even make sense to talk about it in those terms.

In addition, the relationship between smoking and cancer shows all of the effects that would be expected if smoking causes cancer. The more cigarettes people smoke, the more likely they are to get cancer; the more years they smoke, the more likely they are to get cancer; if they stop smoking, their risk of cancer decreases. In contrast, there is no evidence that the more years people are exposed to violent television, the more aggressive they are; or that if they stop watching violent television, they become less aggressive. These so called dose-response effects are crucial for the scientific case to be made, and they simply do not exist.

Some critics claim that the link between television violence and violent behavior is as clear and evident as the link between smoking and lung cancer.

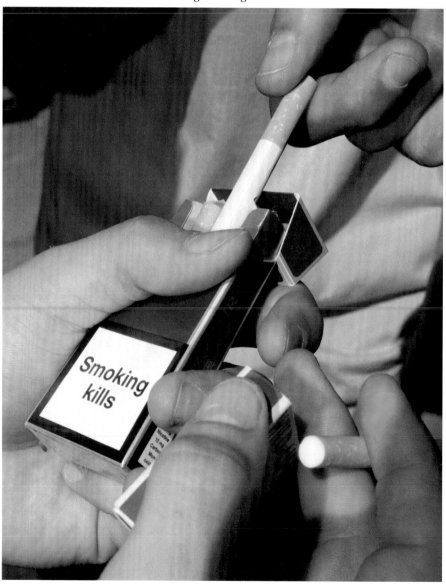

Making Predictions

Having raised the issue of smoking and cancer, let me use it to contrast what the real world tells us about that and about television violence and aggression. If smoking causes lung cancer, there should be observable effects on real people living in the real world. It is not enough to show that smokers are more likely to get lung cancer, because there might conceivably be other explanations for that. However, we can make more precise predictions.

In the early part of the 20th century, most women in the United States did not smoke because it was not considered proper. We should therefore expect that during that period, the rate of lung cancer in men should have been much higher than in women. It was! Later in the century, attitudes changed and women began to smoke. We should expect that the rates of lung cancer in women would begin to go up and eventually become close to those in men. They did! In other words, what occurred in the real world was just what we would expect if smoking caused lung cancer. This is not definitive proof of the effect, but if we had not seen this relationship, it sure would have made us wonder and perhaps question our assumption about smoking and cancer.

The Crime Rate

How about television violence? If it causes people to be more aggressive, we should expect that to show up in rates of violent crime. About 10 years after television was introduced into the United States, the rate of violent crime began to go up and increased dramatically from 1965 to 1980. One possible explanation was that the increase was caused by exposure to television violence. The explanation of the time-lag for the increase was that the effect would be mainly on children, and that it would take several years until they got old enough to begin committing violent crimes. So when the crime rate began to increase, many people blamed it on television. Of course, many other factors could have caused the increase, but television was a convenient (though I would say implausible) target.

However, it is incumbent on those blaming television to follow through on their analysis. After about 1980 the rate of violent crime leveled off in the United States until about 1992. At that point, we

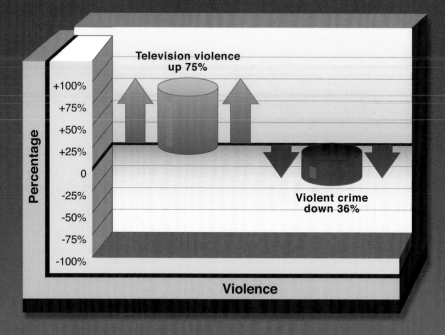

Changes in Television Violence and Violent Crime, 1998–2005

Television violence up 75%

Violent crime down 36%

Percentage

+100%
+75%
+50%
+25%
0
-25%
-50%
-75%
-100%

Violence

Taken from: Caroline Schulenburg, "Dying to Entertain: Violence on Prime Time Broadcast Television, 1998 to 2006," Parents Television Council, January 2007. www.parentstv.org/ptc/publications/reports/violencestudy/exsummary.asp. Bureau of Justice Statistics, "Criminal Victimization in the United States Statistical Table," U.S. Department of Justice, 1998 and 2005. www.ojp.usdoj.gov/bjs/abstract/cvusst.htm.

still had lots of violent programming on television, we had vivid and more and more realistic violence in films, we had violent lyrics in rap music, and we had the rapidly growing popularity of video games, especially violent video games being played by young males. If violent television causes aggression, and if (as many of the same people believe) violent movies, violent lyrics in rap music, and violent video games cause aggression, the rate of violent crime should have gone through the roof.

That did not happen. Instead, there was a sharp decline in violent crime that started in 1992 and continued to the point that the rate is now below what it was before television became popular. And just to be clear, this was not due to a change in demographics, since the drop in violent crime rate was particularly sharp among young males who are the ones who commit a disproportionate number of such crimes.

This by itself, though clearly inconsistent with the causal hypothesis, does not disprove it. Many other explanations of the pattern are possible. But surely it must make those who favor the hypothesis, and who blamed television for the earlier increase, wonder why we did not see the pattern they should have predicted. It should also give pause to those legislators who are concerned about the harmful effects of television violence. They should ask themselves why, if television is so harmful, there is less violent crime now than there was when they were young. . . .

In sum, there is no convincing scientific evidence that television violence causes children to be aggressive, or that any particular depiction of violence on television has this effect, or that it affects any particular type of children more than others. There has been a considerable amount of research on this topic—enough so that if there were an effect, the research should have shown it. Therefore, my conclusion is that either there is no effect of television violence on aggression, or, if there is an effect, it is vanishingly small because otherwise the research would have found it.

EVALUATING THE AUTHOR'S ARGUMENTS:

In this viewpoint Jonathan L. Freedman claims that a decline in violent crime in the years following the huge growth in violent media proves that media violence does not cause actual violence. How might Dale Kunkel, the author of the previous viewpoint, address this claim in order to defend his view?

Chapter 3

Should the Government Regulate Violent Media?

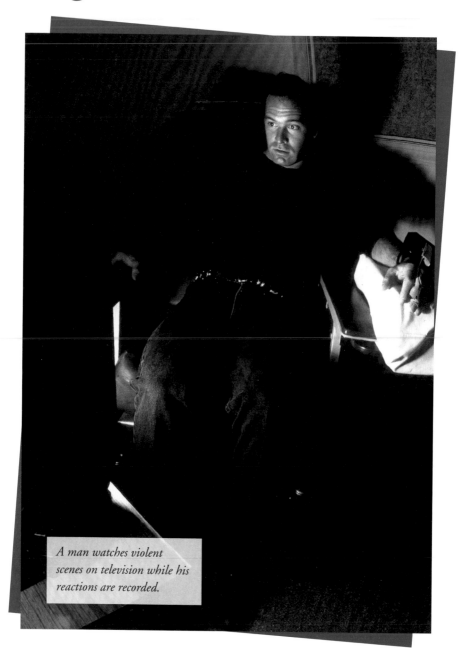

A man watches violent scenes on television while his reactions are recorded.

The First Amendment Protects Video Games from Regulation

Marjorie Heins

"Violent expression is generally protected by the First Amendment unless the government can show a 'compelling' reason for its suppression."

In the following viewpoint Marjorie Heins discusses video game censorship laws that have been pursued by several states and localities in recent years. She argues that the propensity to blame media violence for juvenile delinquency has a long history. Heins contends that an attempt in 2000 to link video game violence with aggression is seriously flawed. She notes that several courts around the country have also found such evidence lacking, thus striking down video game censorship laws for lack of a compelling justification necessary to restrict the First Amendment right to free expression. Heins is an activist, a writer, and the founder of the Free Expression Policy Project, an organization providing research and advocacy on free speech, copyright, and media democracy issues.

AS YOU READ, CONSIDER THE FOLLOWING QUESTIONS:
  1. According to Heins, the history of media violence politics goes back how far?
  2. The author discusses an ordinance in St. Louis that restricted minors' access to violent video games. Which court struck down this law?
  3. According to the author, the California law restricting violent video games banned distribution to minors of games that did one of what two things?

The August 6, 2007 decision by U.S. District Judge Ronald Whyte striking down California's video game censorship law was the ninth such ruling by a federal court in the past six years. Yet state and local legislators continue to press for laws restricting minors' access to games with "violence," "inappropriate violence," "ultra violence," or whatever other term they hope will ban the games they think harmful.

According to the website Game Censorship.com, Delaware, Indiana, Kansas, New York, North Carolina, and Utah are currently considering legislation restricting minors' access to games with violent content. The nine states or localities whose laws have been struck down include (in addition to California) Indianapolis, St. Louis, Michigan, Washington, Illinois, Louisiana, Minnesota, and Oklahoma.

The Politics of Media Violence

Why do lawmakers continue to press for censorship of video games despite the clear unconstitutionality of the enterprise? The answer probably lies in the long history of media-violence politics, a history that goes back more than a century, to an era when concerns that crime and detective magazines would corrupt urban youth first led to laws banning stories of "bloodshed, lust, or crime." The concern resurfaced in the 1930s, once movies captured the national imagination, and again in the 1950s when television became our dominant mass medium, while crime-and-adventure comics were accused of causing juvenile delinquency. In the 1960s, 70s, and 80s, the government liberally funded researchers who sought to prove harmful effects from gunslinger shows and other televised violence, and politicians as well as the researchers often misrepresented the dubious results of their experiments.

Fast forward to 2000, when four professional associations issued a "Joint Statement" asserting that "well over 1000 studies . . . point overwhelmingly to a causal connection between media violence and aggressive behavior in some children." The Statement was so rife with errors that it was difficult to understand how these groups—which included the American Medical Association (the AMA)—could have endorsed it.

Dr. Edward Hill, chair-elect of the AMA, shed some light on this question the following year during a panel discussion. Responding to questions about the Joint Statement, Dr. Hill explained that it was the AMA's desire for health education funding that drove its support of the Joint Statement. The AMA is "sometimes used by the politicians. We try to balance that because we try to use them also, so it's a contest. . . . There were political reasons for signing on. We're looking for a champion in Congress that will be willing to back our desire for funding for comprehensive school health in this country."

Video Games and Aggression

By the late 1990s, violent video games were stirring new concerns. Their interactivity, some critics said, increased the risk of imitative behavior. Psychologist Craig Anderson became a prominent spokesman for this view; among his experimental findings were that subjects who had played violent games in a laboratory administered slightly longer "noise blasts" than a control group. They also recognized "aggressive words" slightly more quickly. (The difference was in fractions of a second.) Anderson posited that recognizing aggressive words reflects aggressive thoughts, and that aggressive thoughts lead to aggressive behavior.

Anderson's research may have been squishy, but several states and localities relied on it between 2000 and 2006 in passing laws to restrict minors' access to video games. St. Louis's ordinance, for example, criminalized selling, renting, or otherwise making available to minors any "graphically violent" video game, or permitting free play of such a game without the consent of a parent or guardian. The St. Louis County Council, before passing the law, heard testimony from Anderson that playing violent games for 10 to 15 minutes causes "aggressive behavior" and "that children have more aggressive thoughts and frequently more aggressive behavior after playing violent video games."

A federal district court relied on these statements in upholding the law, but the Court of Appeals reversed, finding the County's conclusions to be "simply unsupported in the record." Anderson's "vague generality" about aggressive thoughts and behavior, the judges said, "falls far short of a showing that video games are psychologically deleterious," and other testimony was equally "ambiguous, inconclusive, or irrelevant."

A Lack of Proof

The judges in the St. Louis case cited a decision from a sister court, striking down Indianapolis's ordinance. In that case, the court observed that from Grimm's fairy tales to horror movies and epic poems, violent themes have been part of children's literature; to shield them from the subject "would not only be quixotic [idealistic and unrealistic], but deforming." Neither Anderson's "aggressive word" and "noise blast" experiments nor any other evidence before the court showed that video games "have ever caused anyone to commit a violent act," or "have caused the average level of violence to increase anywhere."

In the Illinois case, the judge was particularly skeptical of expert witness testimony from Anderson and another psychologist, William Kronenberger. The judge noted that Anderson had acknowledged exaggerating the significance of studies that simply show a correlation between aggression and video game play (rather than a causative relationship); that the longer noise blasts his subjects gave after playing violent games were "a matter of milliseconds"; and that he had manipulated the data and methodology in his "meta-analyses." More credible, the court found, were the plaintiffs' experts, who testified that Anderson "not only had failed to cite any peer-reviewed studies that had shown a definitive causal

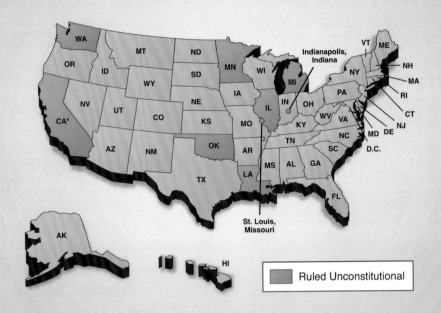

Cities and States Where Laws Restricting Minors' Access to Video Games Were Ruled Unconstitutional

Ruled Unconstitutional

*Indicates cases on appeal as of May 2010.

Taken from: Lawrence G. Walters, GameCensorship.com, November 2009. www.gamecensorship.com/legislation.htm.
Media Coalition, www.mediacoalition.org/FCC-PROPOSAL-TO-REGULATE-VIOLENT-CONTENT.

link between violent video game play and aggression, but had also ignored research that reached conflicting conclusions." The judge was equally unsparing in his dissection of Dr. Kronenberger's testimony that studies of adolescent brain activity point to harm from violent video games.

None of this means, of course, that some violent media might not sometimes reinforce violent attitudes in some people, or even, occasionally, contribute to violent behavior. A lack of proof in court is simply that—a lack of proof. It doesn't mean that the contrary has been proven. Certainly, there are isolated instances of direct imitation, and certainly, the sadistic or misogynistic ideas found in some games are disturbing. As the court decisions suggest, though, it's impossible to define what kind of violent images are harmful (just as it's impossible to pinpoint or quantify violent entertainment's possibly positive effects in relieving tension or processing aggressive feelings in a safe way).

The California Law

The California law was typical in its (unsuccessful) attempt to craft a definition of "violent video game" that wouldn't be so broad as to encompass the universe of historical, sports, fantasy, sci-fi, action/adventure, knights-in-armor, simulated battlefield, or classic literature games. The definition had two parts: it banned distribution to minors of games that either (1) enable players to inflict virtual injury "in a manner which is especially heinous, cruel, or depraved," or that (2) "appeal to a deviant or morbid interest of minors," are "patently offensive to prevailing standards in the community as to what is suitable for minors," and "lack serious literary, artistic, political, or scientific value for minors."

That latter definition was borrowed from the familiar three-part test that courts have used to condemn sexual material that's deemed "obscene" or "harmful to minors." But as Judge Whyte explained, violent expression is generally protected by the First Amendment unless the government can show a "compelling" reason for its suppression; "obscene" sexual expression is not. As for the alternative definition ("heinous, cruel, or depraved"), he pointed out that it "has no exception for material with some redeeming value and is therefore too broad. The definition could literally apply to some classic literature if put in the form of a video game."

California governor Arnold Schwarzenegger was the defendant when the U.S. district court decided that California's video game censorship law violated the First Amendment.

Despite the impossibility of drafting a video game censorship law that wouldn't be unconstitutionally vague and overbroad, politics will likely continue to drive this debate—at least until health professionals, legislators, and other policymakers agree to unite behind programs of media literacy education and genuine violence reduction rather than attacking entertainment and expression. Action-hero-turned-Governor Arnold Schwarzenegger, the defendant in the California case, would be an ideal candidate to lead such an initiative.

Viewpoint

2

The First Amendment Does Not Protect Violent Video Games from Regulation

Phyllis Schlafly

"It is not a First Amendment right to cause panic on an airplane by shouting that someone has a bomb; nor is it legitimate free speech to evoke violent reactions in children through graphic video games."

In the following viewpoint Phyllis Schlafly argues against several court decisions finding that the First Amendment prevents cities and states from having ordinances restricting minors' access to violent video games. She disagrees with the comparison between violent video games and violence in literature—including the Bible—noting what she takes to be key differences between reading the Bible or great literature and playing video games. Schlafly denies that the First Amendment protects violent video games and contends that judges are overstepping their role by finding that it does. Schlafly is a conservative activist and attorney and the author of *The Supremacists: The Tyranny of Judges and How to Stop It.*

AS YOU READ, CONSIDER THE FOLLOWING QUESTIONS:

1. The author disputes a court comparison between violent video games and violence in the Bible, claiming what key difference?
2. Schlafly reports that the court in *American Amusement Machine Association v. Kendrick* compared violent video games to what three works of literature?
3. The author contends that a teenager who learns how to murder and mutilate human beings in video games is desensitized to do what?

Extremely violent video games have become the dangerous obsession of a significant portion of our youth, and several towns and states have passed ordinances intended to prevent minors from buying or viewing them. But judicial supremacists are striking down these laws by claiming this extremely graphic violence deserves the same First Amendment protection as [works by playwright William] Shakespeare.

FAST FACT

According to market research by the NPD Group, nearly 63 percent of Americans have played a video game in the past six months compared with only 53 percent who report going out to the movies in the same time period.

Recent Court Decisions

In March [2008], a three-judge panel for the 8th U.S. Circuit Court of Appeals unanimously held that violent video games are entitled to as much protection as the Bible. This was the ruling of *Entertainment Software Association v. Swanson,* even though one of the video games, *Postal 2: Apocalypse Weekend,* boasts it will enable the user "to hack your enemies to meaty bits!"

Judge Roger L. Wollman, writing for the court, observed that "great literature includes many themes and descriptions of violence. . . ." What Wollman failed to add is that a literary description of violence in the Bible does not engage a teenager in role-playing or desensitize him to the harm.

Interactive Digital Software Association v. St. Louis County likewise held that violent video games are free speech because they contain "stories, imagery, age-old themes of literature, and messages, even an ideology, just as books and movies do." But so do some adult pornographic movies, and no one insists there is a First Amendment right to sell them to children.

That decision acknowledged a psychologist's expert testimony that violent video games frequently lead to aggressive behavior, yet inexplicably rejected it, noting instead that a high school principal who testified was unable to prove that violent video games cause psychological harm to teens who play them.

Video Games and Literature

A similar decision by the 7th U.S. Circuit Court of Appeals, *American Amusement Machine Association v. Kendrick*, considered an ordinance

Conservative activist Phyllis Schlafly believes that the First Amendment does not protect violent video game content, but the courts so far have disagreed.

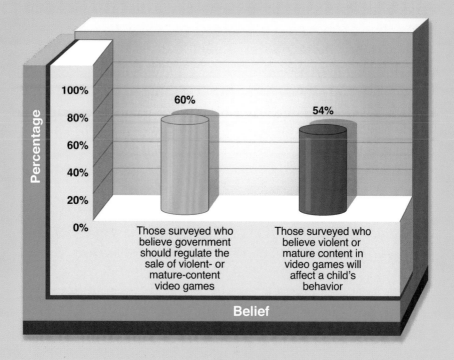

Americans Opinions on Violent Video Games

Percentage

| | 60% | 54% |

Those surveyed who believe government should regulate the sale of violent- or mature-content video games

Those surveyed who believe violent or mature content in video games will affect a child's behavior

Belief

Taken from: Chris Kohler, "Poll: Majority of Americans Think Government Should Regulate Game Content," Wired, December 5, 2007. www.wired.com/gamelife/2007/12/poll-majority-o.

that would have prevented arcade owners with five or more games deemed "harmful to minors" from allowing children to play the games without parental supervision. That court struck down the ordinance, commenting that the violent arcade games in question were not proven to be similar to the standard video games that have been linked to violence, and therefore not directly proven to have harmful effects.

The decision compared violent video games to classic works of literature such as *The Odyssey, The Divine Comedy* and *War and Peace.* There is a distinct difference between sympathizing with the perpetrator of violence and being the perpetrator of violence, but that difference was apparently lost on the court.

In a case involving a video game that shows teenagers how to kill policemen, federal district court Judge Robert S. Lasnik permanently enjoined Washington State from restricting the distribution of violent video games to minors. In *Video Software Dealers Association v. Maleng*, he quoted the *Interactive Digital Software* decision in ruling that "guided by the First Amendment, we are obliged to recognize that they are as much entitled to the protection of free speech as the best of literature."

The First Amendment

These decisions ignore the way violent video games encourage role-playing, making the child the perpetrator of violence in a manner that no book or movie can. It does not require a leap in imagination to see the risk of immature players transferring violent role-playing to real life.

Legitimate free speech expresses violence in a rational context, rather than displaying it graphically to evoke an immediate emotional reaction. It is not a First Amendment right to cause panic on an airplane by shouting that someone has a bomb; nor is it legitimate free speech to evoke violent reactions in children through graphic video games.

A teenager who learns how to murder and mutilate human beings in video games is desensitized to commit heinous crimes against his neighbors. Nothing in the First Amendment should prevent regulations to stop this, supremacist judges to the contrary notwithstanding.

EVALUATING THE AUTHOR'S ARGUMENTS:

In this viewpoint Phyllis Schlafly contends that there is a "risk of immature players transferring violent role-playing to real life." How would Marjorie Heins, the author of the previous viewpoint, respond to the reasoning Schlafly gives for this conclusion?

The Government Should Consider Regulating Television Violence

Caroline Schulenburg

In the following viewpoint Caroline Schulenburg contends that there is widespread agreement and evidence that violent entertainment causes aggression in children. She argues that the only solution offered so far, the V-chip which allows parents to block programs with certain ratings, is not properly used or understood. Even with proper use, Schulenburg believes it is not a solution because of the inaccurate ratings used by broadcast networks. She proposes that advertisers and broadcast affiliates put pressure on the networks for a reduction in violent programming, and she urges lawmakers to consider government regulation of television violence. Schulenburg is an analyst for the Parents Television Council, an organization advocating responsible entertainment.

"Perhaps it is time for Congress to revisit this issue and consider including violence in the category of 'indecent' content that can be regulated by the Federal Communications Commission."

Caroline Schulenburg, "Dying to Entertain: Violence on Prime Time Broadcast Television, 1998 to 2006," Alexandria, VA: Parents Television Council, 2007. Copyright © 2007 Parents Television Council. Reproduced by permission.

AS YOU READ, CONSIDER THE FOLLOWING QUESTIONS:

1. According to the author, what percentage of adults believes portrayals of violence in popular culture contribute to violent behavior in teens?
2. Schulenburg cites a Zogby poll that found what percentage of respondents able to correctly identify the content descriptors used by the television industry to rate programs?
3. What proportion of television shows, according to the author, was found by the Kaiser Family Foundation to contain violent or sexual behavior but without the proper content descriptors?

I n a survey published in the *Christian Science Monitor*, adults cited television as the cause of teenage violence above lack of supervision, parents, breakdown of family, or drugs. Fifty-six percent of adults surveyed said that portrayals of violence in popular culture contribute to violent behavior in teens. Medical professionals agree. In a 2004 survey of pediatricians, over 98% believe that the media affect childhood aggression.

The Need for a Solution

Violence on television continues unabated despite the overwhelming evidence pointing to a direct and causal relationship between violent entertainment products and aggressive behavior in children. As computer graphics and special effects evolve and become more sophisticated, we can expect television violence to become more explicit and increasingly realistic.

> **FAST FACT**
>
> According to the Parents Television Council, 49 percent of all television episodes on broadcast television aired during the 2005–2006 season during the evening hours, contained at least one instance of violence.

Yet the only solution offered up by the entertainment industry thus far has been the V-Chip [which allows parents to block programs with certain ratings]. But the V-Chip is no solution.

Parents' Views on Regulation

Percent of parents who favor new regulations to limit the amount of sex and violence in television shows during the early evening hours:

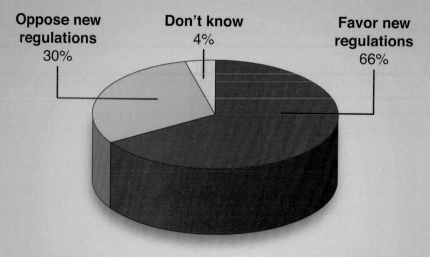

Oppose new regulations 30%

Don't know 4%

Favor new regulations 66%

Taken from: Kaiser Family Foundation, "Parents, Children, and Media: A Kaiser Family Foundation Survey," June 2007. www.kff.org.

A June 2000 study conducted by the Annenberg Public Policy Center at the University of Pennsylvania found that only half of parents were even aware of the television ratings. Only 39% reported using the ratings to guide their children's viewing. More than a third had never heard of the V-Chip.

Problems with the V-Chip

Would raising awareness of the V-Chip help? The Annenberg Center also conducted an experiment from 1999–2001 in which they provided families with young children with V-Chip equipped television sets and tracked their response to the device over a one-year period. Out of the 110 families who received V-Chip equipped television sets, 70% reported they never used the V-Chip during the one-year period. In a more recent survey conducted by Zogby on behalf of the Parents Television Council [PTC], 87% of respondents reported that they had not used the V-Chip or cable box parental controls to block unwanted content from their television in the previous week.

The biggest obstacle to families using the V-Chip was lack of awareness of the ratings and the V-Chip. This is corroborated by a July 2001 national survey by the Kaiser Family Foundation which found that even among those who have heard of the ratings system, many parents don't understand what those ratings mean. Only 7% of respondents to the Zogby poll could correctly identify the content descriptors used by the TV industry to rate programs—even when provided with the correct answers.

The Ratings System

But even if there were universal awareness of the V-Chip and the ratings system, how useful would this technology really be?

The PTC's research shows that every broadcast network has had problems with the accurate and consistent application of content descriptors (D, S, L, or V [(suggestive) dialogue, sexual situations,

The entertainment industry introduced the V-chip, which has been used to block TV programs with violent content. Critics say it has been the only solution offered by the industry.

language, or violence]) which were added to the ratings system after complaints that the earlier, age-based ratings system was too vague. It is these content descriptors that are supposed to work in conjunction with the V-Chip to help parents block objectionable programming.

A study by the Kaiser Family Foundation found that content descriptors are not being used on the vast majority of general audience shows containing sex, violence, or adult language. Eight out of 10 television shows with violent or sexual behavior did not receive the V or S content descriptors. Children's programs also contain a significant amount of violence, most of which is not indicated by a FV [fantasy violence] content descriptor.

A Better Solution

Clearly, we need a better solution.

Advertisers have a role to play in curbing TV violence. Using their unique position of influence, they can encourage broadcasters to reduce the frequency and explicitness of TV violence.

Broadcast affiliates, too, can play a role by preempting excessively violent programs and refusing to air violent programs in syndication during times of day when children are watching TV.

Many lawmakers have proposed legislation to curb TV violence, but all attempts to legislatively address this problem have failed on First Amendment grounds. Perhaps it is time for Congress to revisit this issue and consider including violence in the category of "indecent" content that can be regulated by the Federal Communications Commission.

EVALUATING THE AUTHOR'S ARGUMENTS:

In this viewpoint Caroline Schulenburg advocates that Congress consider regulation of television violence by the Federal Communications Commission. Why does Nick Gillespie, the author of the next viewpoint, think this is a bad idea?

Viewpoint
4

"It's safe to say that when a quartet of do-gooder, pizza-chomping cartoon reptiles has become a predicate for federal regulation, American governance has gone seriously off the rails."

The Government Should Not Regulate Violent Television Programming

Nick Gillespie

In the following viewpoint Nick Gillespie argues that a 2007 report by the Federal Communications Commission calling for government regulation of violent television is misguided. Gillespie accuses the report's authors of justifying regulation based on bad science: He claims that no science has supported the link between media violence and violent behavior. Gillespie points to a wide variety of controls currently available for parents to block certain television shows from their homes and concludes that the low utilization of these tools proves that governmental regulation is not needed. Gillespie is the editor in chief of Reason.tv and Reason.com, both productions of the Reason Foundation, a national nonprofit libertarian research and educational organization.

Nick Gillespie, "The FCC's Not Our Mommy and Daddy," *Los Angeles Times*, May 2, 2007, p. A23.
Copyright © 2007 Los Angeles Times. Reproduced by permission of the author.

Should the Government Regulate Violent Media?   93

AS YOU READ, CONSIDER THE FOLLOWING QUESTIONS:
1. Gillespie claims that juvenile violent crime arrests have dropped steadily for how many years?
2. The author accuses members of the Federal Communications Commission of speaking not as social scientists in their report, but as what?
3. Gillespie claims that what percentage of parents regularly uses parental controls such as the V-chip or cable channel blockers?

A t the behest of Congress, the Federal Communications Commission [FCC] issued a report last week [April 25, 2007,] on "violent television programming and its impact on children" that calls not just for expanding governmental oversight of broadcast TV but extending content regulation to cable and satellite channels for the first time. The FCC also recommended that some shows be banned from time slots when children might be watching and that cable and satellite operators be forced to offer "a la carte" service in which subscribers would pick and choose among individual channels.

FAST FACT

According to Adam Thierer of the Progress and Freedom Foundation, as of 2007 only 32 percent of U.S. households have children in them, with only a subset of this percentage requiring parental control technologies for media.

The Link Between Violent TV and Violence

Despite its sober tone, the study rests on the demonstrably false idea that violent TV breeds violence in reality, and it also fails to take seriously the vast increase in child-friendly programming and parent-empowering viewing tools. The result is a list of recommendations to Congress that seems as comically and absurdly detached from contemporary America as an episode of *SpongeBob SquarePants*.

"America is hooked on violence," laments Commissioner Jonathan S. Adelstein, who ostensibly believes that the FCC's proposed policies would make the United States safer. "Particularly in light of the spasm of unconscionable violence at Virginia Tech [referring to the 2007 school shooting in which thirty-three were killed]," he continues in his statement approving the report, "but just as importantly in light of the excessive violent crime that daily afflicts our nation, there is a basis for appropriate federal action to curb violence in the media."

Yet the report itself cites a 2001 U.S. surgeon general report that concluded "many questions remain regarding the short- and long-term effects of media violence, especially on violent behavior." More to the point, if fantasy violence translates readily into its real-world counterpart, then why have juvenile violent crime arrests dropped steadily for 12 years? According to a 2006 Department of Justice report, such arrests have fallen "to a level not seen since at least the 1970s."

The same trend is true for violent crime among the larger population. There seems little question that depictions of violence in popular culture—including TV, movies, music, video games and more—have become more frequent and more graphic since 1994. If Adelstein's thesis were true, the facts on the ground would be otherwise.

The Time-Scout Monitor by Card Access, Inc., is designed to monitor a child's computer time.

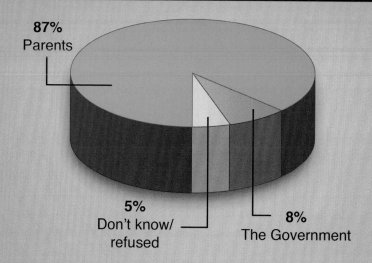

Views on Television Regulation

Who do you think would do a better job of protecting children from violent and offensive content on television?

87%
Parents

5%
Don't know/
refused

8%
The Government

Taken from: TV Watch Topline, June 2007, Luntz, Maslansky Strategic Research & Heart Research.
www.televisionwatch.org.

A Parental Concern

But the FCC commissioners speak less as social scientists and more as parents. "I am deeply concerned about the negative effects violent programming appears to have on our children," writes Commissioner Deborah Taylor Tate. "Many of us, as parents, have witnessed our children acting out a fighting scene from an episode of *Teenage Mutant Ninja Turtles* . . . or been awakened by a frightened child climbing into bed after having a nightmare because of something they saw on television."

The ultimate goal of the report, she argues, is not simply to empower parents who worry about what's on TV in their house but to change "the media landscape *outside* our homes" (emphasis hers) and to increase "the amount of family-friendly, uplifting and nonviolent programming being produced."

It's safe to say that when a quartet of do-gooder, pizza-chomping cartoon reptiles has become a predicate for federal regulation, American governance has gone seriously off the rails. Similarly, if the FCC is in the business of banning children's nightmares, look for the agency to go after circus clowns any day now.

The Rise in Parental Control

More to the point, the FCC seems to be wholly unaware that, in recent years, cable TV has become jampacked with channels dedicated to the sort of fare Tate demands. Nickelodeon, Cartoon Network, Disney Kids, Sprout, Noggin and others devote most or all of their hours to kid-friendly culture.

At the same time, parents have gained unprecedented control over the tube. Since 2000, all new TV sets have come equipped with a government-mandated "V-chip," which allows parents to automatically block specific programs based on violence, language or sexual content ratings. The typical TV or cable/satellite box includes other controls as well that allow the blocking of channels and restrict access to the set. And, of course, all TVs come with an on/off switch. (Though as FCC Chairman Kevin J. Martin, perhaps channeling TV's laziest father, Homer Simpson, said in 2005: "You can always turn the television off and, of course, block the channels you don't want. . . . But why should you have to?") The report notes all this but assumes that the low usage rates of such tools—only about 12% of parents report regularly using the V-chip or cable channel blockers—mean that parents' wishes are being thwarted rather than fulfilled.

Maybe. But in a report that systematically misreads contemporary America, it's more likely that the FCC is simply mistaken.

> **EVALUATING THE AUTHOR'S ARGUMENTS:**
>
> In this viewpoint Nick Gillespie claims that the low use of controls such as the V-chip supports the conclusion that people do not want or need more regulation. How might Caroline Schulenburg and Paul M. Weyrich, authors of other viewpoints in this chapter, disagree with this conclusion?

A la Carte Cable Programming Is Necessary to Avoid Regulation of Violent Television

"Let parents choose which channels their children should see and pay only for those channels."

Paul M. Weyrich

In the following viewpoint Paul M. Weyrich argues that in order to avoid government regulation of violent television, the cable companies need to offer a la carte programming, which would let consumers choose the channels they want to watch and pay only for those channels. Weyrich claims that television violence is rampant and poses a risk to children who are watching far too much television. Weyrich urges parents to have their children watch less television, and he denies that the V-chip is an effective tool for parental control over objectionable content when the television is on. The only way to avoid government regulation, he concludes, is to allow people

Paul M. Weyrich, "A la Carte Cable Programming Needed," *Washington Times*, May 13, 2007, p. A17. Reproduced by permission.

to have control over what channels come into their homes. Weyrich (1942–2008) was an American conservative activist and commentator who founded two conservative think tanks: the Heritage Foundation and the Free Congress Foundation.

AS YOU READ, CONSIDER THE FOLLOWING QUESTIONS:
1. According to Nielsen Media, the television is on in the American home for an average of how many hours a day?
2. What percentage of American households, according to the author, pays for cable or satellite television?
3. Weyrich claims that cable companies have increased their rates by how much over the last ten years?

Violence on television has been increasing at an alarming rate. On any given evening on network or cable there are countless murders, beatings and torture scenes in almost every dramatic show. Many people, and especially parents of small children, are fed up with this situation and for several years there has been talk of limiting the violence and the so-called "adult" language on television by federal law. Considering this possibility in 2004, the 109th Congress requested a study of the effects of violent television programming on children from the Federal Communications Commission (FCC). The report is now complete and the findings are not pretty.

In results similar to those already determined by the Surgeon General's office, the American Medical Association, the Kaiser Family Foundation and several other sponsors of previous studies on the topic, the FCC found that television violence is pervasive and nearly unavoidable. This is the case late in the evening and also during the formerly "Family Friendly Hours" of 7–9 P.M. The report concludes that television violence is "linked" to aggressive behavior in children and that it desensitizes them to fighting and makes them more fearful as well.

Part of the problem is that we have become a nation of television addicts and we are passing the addiction on to our children. One study by Nielsen Media, the company that invented the original

Steve Kelley Editorial Cartoon used with the permission of Steve Kelley and Creators Syndicate.

television ratings system, determined that a television is on in the American home an average of 8 hours and 11 minutes every day.

As the father of five grown children and a longtime veteran of the culture wars, I was astonished at that figure. Have things gotten so far out of whack in the American family? I realize we no longer live in the era of "Leave It To Beaver" and "The Andy Griffith Show." Many mothers have to work or want to work outside the home and more and more children have no fathers to speak of. Every day I see additional evidence that the traditional family unit of one mother and one father who are actually married to each other and live with their own children ought to be put on the endangered species list along with the spotted owl and the kangaroo rat. However, I did not realize that the television set had become the equivalent of a parent. For it to be on that long suggests that there are many households in which it has taken the place of playing with children, reading to them, eating [with] or even talking to them.

It is not surprising that the great majority of U.S. households pay for some form of television services via cable or satellite. Somewhere between 70 percent and 85 percent of American households, depending on which study you read, pay for cable or satellite television. "Basic" cable, as it is called in most regions of the country, or "premium" cable or a satellite dish are in the majority of our homes for a variety of reasons. Many consumers really want to choose from 80 or more channels; others would be happy with 10 or fewer. The average home watches only 17 of the channels it receives in a premium cable package, and in certain areas of the country paying for cable is the only way to get any television reception at all. (This is especially true in large cities where the density of the population and the number of tall buildings makes it nearly impossible for the analog signal to get to a television set.)

For the last decade the cable industry has been promoting the V-chip, which allows parents to block objectionable programming when the television is on. The V-chip sounds like a good idea but it is yet another example of the consumer paying more money for less service and then doing most of the work. First, the consumer must make sure the television set was made after 2000; older sets do not have the V-chip capability. The adult must then learn how to program the V-system and hope that the children don't figure out how to override their parent's password. As there frequently is more than one TV in the average house, each TV must be programmed for the V-chip to work.

Then there are the so-called V-chip ratings, which are based

FAST FACT

According to a 2006 survey by the Kaiser Family Foundation, 18 percent of parents do not have a V-chip-equipped television, and 57 percent of those who have a V-chip-equipped television do not know they have a V-chip.

on age groups. The guidelines include letters such as "L" for language and "D" for dialogue and "V" for violence, but these guidelines are confusing, open to interpretation and done by the television programmers themselves. That's right; the shows are rated by the people who want you to watch them.

Wouldn't it be simpler if Americans could simply pick the stations we want and not take the channels we do not? Unfortunately, the cable industry has made this impossible. Consumers must pay for premium rather than basic cable simply to get one or two channels they want such as Fox News or American Movie Classics. They pay between $50 and $80 per month and take an entire "bundle" of channels when they only watch one or two. The cable companies have insisted for many years that "unbundling" the channels is impractical if not impossible, even though it works quite well in other countries, such as Canada.

Before advocating that the government or the FCC step in and regulate, we must first fulfill our responsibilities as parents. Turn off the television set (or sets). That should be obvious to every parent of every religion or philosophical belief. No child should be watching two to four hours of television every night.

As for the cable companies, I have little sympathy. They have greatly contributed to lowering the standards of decency in television programming and have increased their rates an average of 90 percent over the last 10 years. If they want to forestall regulation,

Proponents of parental controls think that cable TV companies should offer their customers a la carte programming.

they need to offer a la carte programming. Let the market work and "debundle." Let parents choose which channels their children should see and pay only for those channels. We may not be able to bring back the days of June and Ward Cleaver, but we should be able to keep violent and disgusting television programs out of our own homes.

EVALUATING THE AUTHOR'S ARGUMENTS:

In this viewpoint Paul M. Weyrich claims that the difficulty in programming the V-chip, coupled with V-chip ratings being produced by television programmers themselves, makes obvious the need for a la carte cable programming. Would Nick Gillespie, the author of the previous viewpoint, approve of Weyrich's solution to television violence? Why or why not?

More Information About Television Is Preferable to Regulation

Gene Policinski

"*More and better information for parents and others to use in deciding what programs to watch puts decision-making in the hands of citizens, not censors.*"

In the following viewpoint Gene Policinski argues that government regulation of violent television should be avoided. He discusses a possible difficulty with government regulation by citing examples of violent programs that presumably people would not want censored. Policinski claims that Americans do not want government regulation but simply want more information. He concludes that offering more thorough programming information is vastly preferable to government regulation. Policinski is the vice president and executive director of the First Amendment Center, a forum for the study and exploration of free-expression issues.

AS YOU READ, CONSIDER THE FOLLOWING QUESTIONS:
1. According to the author, a new report by the Federal Communications Commission (FCC) suggests that Congress may wish to extend its regulatory authority to what?
2. Policinski cites surveys by the First Amendment Center that found that 80 percent of Americans believe what party should be primarily responsible for what is on the television screen?
3. The author criticizes the FCC for wanting to act against violent programming for what reason?

How do you cut down on TV violence without doing violence to free expression?

The impact of violence airing on home screens is not a new subject, but some new thinking—and not a little discussion as a result—has come recently from the Federal Communications Commission [FCC], national watchdog over the public airwaves.

The FCC commissioners increasingly have focused in recent years on preventing or punishing what they deem indecent sexual images or utterances on broadcast television. Think fines on broadcasters for Janet Jackson's "wardrobe malfunction," for [U2 singer] Bono's use of the f-word in a live awards telecast, or for various Howard Stern "regular" radio comments deemed objectionable.

The FCC's new [2007] report, *Violent Television Programming and Its Impact on Children*, suggests that Congress may wish—among other options—to extend its regulatory authority to include limits on violent material. But just as with judging sexual imagery and utterances that may be indecent, there are practical problems in defining what depictions of violence cross the line, going from harmless-and-acceptable to dangerous-and-prohibited. And there still is not proven to any great degree a direct link between violence on TV and the causing of actual crime or violent acts.

> **FAST FACT**
>
> The Telecommunications Act of 1996 mandated that the broadcasting industry have a rating system and that television manufacturers install the V-chip by 2000.

According to national surveys in 2004 and 2005, Americans think that parents and TV producers should be responsible for what is seen on TV.

The Marketplace of Ideas

I suspect most agree that torture and bloody carnage are at one end of the socially acceptable spectrum of violent scenes and that purely slapstick Keystone Kops kinds of comedic brutality are at the other. But where on the culture meter should a government body put those popular faux-documentary programs where real police officers are shown using brute force in making actual arrests? However they are defined in television guides, bureaucratic offices or corporate board-rooms, those TV shows certainly are not "news programs" nor are they civics-lesson tutorials on how police agencies function.

And what about blood-and-bash reality shows that purport to be full-contact "sports" events, or professional boxing matches? What about war movies—to say nothing of the real war images from Iraq, Afghanistan and elsewhere? What about private-investigator shows and law-and-order shows and soap operas where someone is always in danger, and . . . well, you get the idea, and perhaps a sense of the difficulty.

In theory, the solution to dealing with TV violence that probably fits the First Amendment best is the "marketplace of ideas": We all move from electronic stall to stall, using the television remote to stuff our viewing bags full. Of course, a real marketplace works because we get to squeeze, sniff and examine the produce before we buy it.

Government Regulation

National surveys in 2004 and 2005 by the First Amendment Center found that Americans see government a distant third—behind parents at 80% and the producers of television programs at 10–15%—as parties that should be primarily responsible in determining what's seen on the family screen.

TV ratings and brief program descriptions are a start. More and better information for parents and others to use in deciding what programs to watch puts decision-making in the hands of citizens, not censors. Specific, accurate information that spells out violent acts

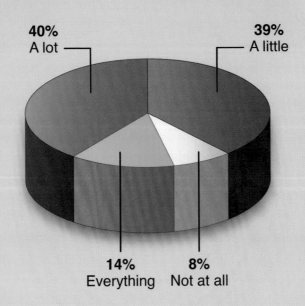

How Much Parents Understand About Television Ratings*

40%
A lot

39%
A little

14%
Everything

8%
Not at all

*Note: Percentages may not add up to 100 due to rounding.

Taken from: The Harris Poll #125, December 14, 2007.

empowers parents and others. And having to be brutally honest about the brutality portrayed at least puts program producers on the public record about the material they present.

Yes, a program guide that notes "one murder, two shootings and one fistfight" may seem ghoulish to some and laughable to others. But it would settle an issue raised by some that parents today can't predict what their children will see in an unregulated environment.

Ironically, the FCC report notes the popularity of violent programming even as it cites that very popularity as one reason to act against it. Sounds a bit like the nation's experiment in Prohibition—and we all know how well that worked. In reality, the media marketplace has demonstrated well that when Americans truly are exercised over something they don't like on "the tube," things happen. . . .

Violence may well be a national turn-off for many parents, political leaders and FCC commissioners. But the public ought to be very careful about handing over the national TV remote control to the heavy hand of government so that it can restrict the free choice of some viewers to tune in.

We ought to remember the words of Jack Paar, acerbic talk-show pioneer and host of the *Tonight Show* in the early 1960s, who once said of censorship, individual choice and television content (in an era when TV sets had dials): "God gave me a mind and a wrist that turns things off."

EVALUATING THE AUTHOR'S ARGUMENTS:

In this viewpoint Gene Policinski argues for more and better information about television programming rather than government regulation. Would Caroline Schulenburg, Nick Gillespie, and Paul M. Weyrich—the other authors in this chapter who discuss television regulation—be in favor of his suggestion? Would any of them raise problems with relying solely on more and better information instead of regulation?

Facts About Media Violence

Editor's note: These facts can be used in reports or papers to reinforce or add credibility when making important points or claims.

Children and Media Consumption

According to a study by the Kaiser Family Foundation of eight- to eighteen-year-olds in 2005:

- Average television consumption per day was three hours and four minutes.
- Twenty percent reported watching more than five hours of television on the previous day.
- Average audio consumption (radio and CDs/MP3s) was one hour and forty-four minutes per day.
- Average computer activity time was one hour and two minutes per day.
- Games constituted an average of 35 percent of computer activity time.
- Average video game consumption was forty-seven minutes per day.
- Average movie consumption was twenty-five minutes per day.
- Average time spent with books was twenty-three minutes per day.
- Average time with magazines was fourteen minutes per day.
- Average time spent with newspapers was six minutes per day.
- Total average media use time was six hours and twenty-one minutes per day.

Parents and Media Control

According to a 2007 Harris poll:

- Thirty-one percent of parents say they argue with their children about when they are allowed to play video games and about the amount of time spent playing video games.
- Nineteen percent of parents argue with their kids about the types of video games they can play.

According to research conducted in 2009 by the Entertainment Software Association:

- Seventy-two percent of parents place time limits on Internet usage.
- Sixty-three percent of parents place time limits on movie viewing.
- Seventy-one percent of parents place time limits on television viewing.
- Seventy-nine percent of parents place time limits on video game playing.
- Ninety-two percent of parents are involved in the purchase or rental of their kids' video games.
- Ninety-four percent of parents say they monitor the content of the games their children play.

According to a survey by the Kaiser Family Foundation in 2006:

- Seventy-seven percent of parents have consulted movie ratings.
- Fifty-three percent of parents have consulted television ratings.
- Fifty-six percent of parents have consulted video game ratings.

Children and Media Equipment

According to a study by the Kaiser Family Foundation of eight- to eighteen-year-olds in 2005:

- Sixty-eight percent have a television in their bedroom.
- Sixty-one percent have a portable music player.
- Fifty-five percent have their own handheld video game.
- Fifty-four percent have a VCR or DVD player in their bedroom.
- Forty-nine percent have video games in their bedroom.
- Thirty-one percent have a computer in their bedroom.

Children and Video Games

According to a survey by the Pew Internet and American Life Project in 2008:

- Ninety-seven percent of teens aged twelve to seventeen play computer, Internet, portable, or console games.
- Fifty percent of teens had played games just the day before.

- Fifty percent of boys named a game with a mature (M) or adults only (A/O) rating as their favorite.

The Link Between Media Violence and Actual Violence

According to a survey of parents by the Kaiser Family Foundation in 2006 (figures are rounded):

- Forty-three percent believe exposure to media violence contributes "a lot" to violent behavior in children.
- Thirty-eight percent believe exposure to media violence contributes "somewhat" to violent behavior in children.
- Fourteen percent believe exposure to media violence contributes "only a little" to violent behavior in children.
- Four percent believe exposure to media violence contributes "not at all" to violent behavior in children.

Organizations to Contact

The editors have compiled the following list of organizations concerned with the issues debated in this book. The descriptions are derived from materials provided by the organizations. All have publications or information available for interested readers. The list was compiled on the date of publication of the present volume; the information provided here may change. Be aware that many organizations take several weeks or longer to respond to inquiries, so allow as much time as possible for the receipt of requested materials.

American Civil Liberties Union (ACLU)
125 Broad St., 18th Fl., New York, NY 10004
(212) 549-2500
e-mail: infoaclu@aclu.org
Web site: www.aclu.org

The ACLU is a national organization that works to defend Americans' civil rights as guaranteed in the U.S. Constitution. The ACLU works in courts, legislatures, and communities to defend First Amendment rights, the right to equal protection, the right to due process, and the right to privacy. The ACLU publishes the semiannual newsletter *Civil Liberties Alert* as well as other publications, including "Reclaiming Our Rights: Declaration of First Amendment Rights and Grievances."

Center for Media Literacy (CML)
23852 Pacific Coast Hwy., #472, Malibu, CA 90265
(310) 456-1225 • fax: (310) 456-0020
e-mail: cml@medialit.org
Web site: www.medialit.org

The CML is an educational organization that works to help children and adults prepare for living and learning in a global media culture. The center works to achieve this goal by translating media literacy research and theory into practical information, training, and educational tools for teachers and youth leaders, parents, and caregivers of children. The

CML publishes a newsletter and many studies and reports, including *What We know About Young Children, TV, and Media Violence.*

Entertainment Software Rating Board (ESRB)
317 Madison Ave., 22nd Fl., New York, NY 10017
(212) 759-0700
Web site: www.esrb.org

The ESRB is a nonprofit self-regulatory body established in 1994 by the Entertainment Software Association to help consumers, especially parents, make informed decisions about the computer and video games they choose. The ESRB assigns computer and video game content ratings, enforces industry-adopted advertising guidelines, and helps ensure responsible online privacy practices for the interactive entertainment software industry. The ESRB publishes many resources aimed at parents with information about video games, including "A Parent's Guide to Video Games: Parental Controls and Online Safety."

Federal Communications Commission (FCC)
445 Twelfth St. SW, Washington, DC 20554
(888) 225-5322 • fax: (866) 418-0232
e-mail: fccinfo@fcc.gov
Web site: www. fcc.gov

The FCC is an independent U.S. government agency charged with regulating interstate and international communications by radio, television, wire, satellite, and cable. The FCC's Enforcement Bureau enforces the federal law that prohibits obscene programming and limits indecent or profane programming. The FCC's Web site contains information about television ratings and has information about how to file a complaint.

First Amendment Center
1207 Eighteenth Ave. South, Nashville, TN 37212
(615) 727-1600
e-mail: info@fac.org
Web site: www.fac.org

The First Amendment Center works to preserve and protect First Amendment freedoms through information and education. The center serves as a forum for the study and exploration of free-expression issues, including freedom of speech, freedom of the press, religious liberty, freedom of assembly, and freedom to petition the government. It has a wide variety of publications available on its Web site, including the overview "Violence & Media."

Freedom Forum
555 Pennsylvania Ave. NW, Washington, DC 20001
(202) 292-6100
e-mail: news@freedomforum.org
Web site: www.freedomforum.org

The Freedom Forum is a nonpartisan foundation dedicated to free press and free speech. The Freedom Forum's First Amendment Center works to preserve and protected First Amendment freedoms through information and education. It publishes the annual report *State of the First Amendment.*

Free Expression Policy Project (FEPP)
170 W. Seventy-sixth St., #301, New York, NY 10023
(212) 496-1311
e-mail: margeheins@verizon.net
Web site: www.fepproject.org

FEPP is a think tank that focuses on upholding artistic and intellectual freedom. FEPP provides research and advocacy on free speech, copyright, and media democracy issues. Available on FEPP's Web site are numerous commentaries on issues of free expression, including "The Disconnect Between Fact and Rhetoric in the World of Media Politics."

Media Coalition
275 Seventh Ave., Ste. 1504, New York, NY 10001
(212) 587-4025 • fax: (212) 587-2436
Web site: www.mediacoalition.org

Media Coalition is an association that defends the First Amendment right to produce and sell books, movies, magazines, recordings, DVDs, videotapes, and video games. Media Coalition represents professional media groups by engaging in legal advocacy, congressional research, and legislative action in support of free expression. Available on its Web site are amicus briefs filed in support of the First Amendment and news on recent First Amendment legislation.

Media Institute
2300 Clarendon Blvd., Ste. 503, Arlington, VA 22201
(703) 243-5700 • fax: (703) 243-8808
e-mail: info@mediainstitute.org
Web site: www.mediainstitute.org

The Media Institute is a nonprofit research foundation that exists to foster three goals: freedom of speech, a competitive media and communications industry, and excellence in journalism. The institute publishes books and monographs, prepares regulatory filings and court briefs, convenes conferences, and sponsors a luncheon series in Washington for journalists and communications executives. The Media Institute has several publications available on its Web site, including the policy paper "Reflections of a First Amendment Advocate."

Morality in Media (MIM)
475 Riverside Dr., Ste. 239, New York, NY 10115
(212) 870-3222 • fax: (212) 870-2765
e-mail: mim@moralityinmedia.org
Web site: www.moralityinmedia.org

MIM is a national nonprofit organization established to combat obscenity and uphold decency standards in the media. MIM works to inform the public about the harms of indecent media and seeks to maintain standards of decency on television and in other media. MIM publishes the quarterly *Morality in Media Newsletter* as well as several articles, including "What the Public Thinks About Sex, Vulgarity, and Violence on Television."

National Coalition Against Censorship (NCAC)
275 Seventh Ave., Ste. 1504, New York, NY 10001
(212) 807-6222 • fax: (212) 807-6245
e-mail: ncac@ncac.org
Web site: www.ncac.org

The NCAC is an alliance of fifty-two participating organizations dedicated to protecting free expression and access to information. It has many projects dedicated to educating the public and protecting free expression, including the Free Expression Policy Project, the Kids' Right to Read Project, the Knowledge Project: Censorship and Science, and the Youth Free Expression Network. Among its publications are several briefs it has filed in response to U.S. Supreme Court cases, including the 2010 case about images of violent animal cruelty, *United States v. Stevens*.

Parents Television Council (PTC)
707 Wilshire Blvd., #2075, Los Angeles, CA 90017
(800) 882-6868 • fax: (213) 403-1301
e-mail: editor@parentstv.org
Web site: www.parentstv.org

The PTC is an advocacy organization whose primary mission is to restore responsibility and decency to the entertainment industry. The PTC seeks to discourage the graphic sexual themes, depictions of gratuitous violence, and profane language in broadcast television through citizen action. Among the PTC's special reports are *Top 10 Best and Worst Advertisers* and *The Alarming Family Hour . . . No Place for Children*.

The Progress and Freedom Foundation
1444 Eye St. NW, Ste. 500, Washington, DC 20005
(202) 289-8928 • fax: (202) 289-6079
e-mail: mail@pff.org
Web site: www.pff.org

The Progress and Freedom Foundation is a market-oriented think tank that studies the digital revolution and its implications for public policy. Its mission is to educate policymakers, opinion leaders, and the public about issues associated with technological change based on a philosophy of limited government, free markets, and individual sovereignty. The Progress and Freedom Foundation publishes the periodicals *Progress on Point, Progress Snapshot,* and the *Skeptical Regulator,* all of which are available on its Web site.

For Further Reading

Books

Anderson, Craig A., Douglas A. Gentile, and Katherine E. Buckley. *Violent Video Game Effects on Children and Adolescents: Theory, Research, and Public Policy.* New York: Oxford University Press, 2007. This work presents an overview of empirical research on the effects of violent video games and then adds to this literature three new studies that fill in the gaps.

Cooper, Cynthia A. *Violence in the Media and Its Influence on Criminal Defense.* Jefferson, NC: McFarland, 2007. The author looks at media violence and its possible influence on young viewers, examining how the "media made me do it" defense has affected today's courtrooms.

Couvares, Francis G., ed. *Movie Censorship and American Culture.* Amherst: University of Massachusetts Press, 2006. Eleven essays examine nearly a century of struggle over cinematic representations of sex, crime, violence, religion, race, and ethnicity, revealing that the effort to regulate the screen has reflected deep social and cultural schisms.

Feldman, Stephen M. *Free Expression and Democracy in America: A History.* Chicago: University of Chicago Press, 2008. This book traces two rival traditions in American culture—suppression of speech and dissent as a form of speech—to provide an overview of the law, history, and politics of individual rights in the United States.

Grimes, Tom, James A. Anderson, and Lori Bergen. *Media Violence and Aggression: Science and Ideology.* Thousand Oaks, CA: Sage, 2008. This work provides information to understand why the hypothesis about aggression due to media violence does not explain or predict how most people react to what they see and hear in the media.

Heins, Marjorie. *Not in Front of the Children: "Indecency," Censorship, and the Innocence of Youth.* Piscataway, NJ: Rutgers University Press, 2007. The author explores the history of indecency laws and other restrictions aimed at protecting youth, with examples from around the globe.

Kirsh, Steven J. *Children, Adolescents, and Media Violence: A Critical Look at the Research.* Thousand Oaks, CA: Sage, 2006. This is a review and critique of the literature related to media violence in all its forms as experienced during childhood and adolescence.

Kutner, Lawrence, and Cheryl Olson. *Grand Theft Childhood: The Surprising Truth About Violent Video Games and What Parents Can Do.* New York: Simon & Schuster, 2008. Recounting the results of their study on the effects of video games, the authors state that their findings conform to the views of neither the alarmists nor the video game industry boosters.

Mitchell, Jolyon. *Media Violence and Christian Ethics.* New York: Cambridge University Press, 2007. This work highlights Christianity's ambiguous relationship with media violence, arguing that Christian practices can provide the context where violence can be remembered and reframed.

Pollard, Tom. *Sex and Violence: The Hollywood Censorship Wars.* Boulder, CO: Paradigm, 2009. This book examines the history and social dynamics of film censorship in the United States, from the beginning of cinema in the 1890s to the present.

Santos, Jody. *Daring to Feel: Violence, the News Media, and Their Emotions.* Lanham, MD: Lexington, 2009. The author challenges the journalistic mandate to remain objective, particularly as it pertains to the emotional topic of violence.

Silverman, David S. *You Can't Air That: Four Cases of Controversy and Censorship in American Television Programming.* Syracuse, NY: Syracuse University Press, 2007. The author assesses four controversial television programs from the perspective of media history, assessing the censorship imposed and the response from broadcast television.

Sternheimer, Karen. *It's Not the Media: The Truth About Pop Culture's Influence on Children.* Boulder, CO: Westview, 2003. This work considers why media culture is a perennial target of both fascination and concern, concluding that fear of social change is the reason we are so often encouraged to believe media culture is the root of many social problems.

Steyer, James P. *The Other Parent: The Inside Story of the Media's Effect on Our Children.* New York: Atria, 2003. This book offers critical guidance for parents for understanding and processing the media reality that children face.

Trend, David. *The Myth of Media Violence: A Critical Introduction.* Malden, MA: Blackwell, 2007. The author assesses current and historical debates over violence in film, television, and video games, extending the conversation beyond simple condemnation or support and addressing a diverse range of issues.

Periodicals and Internet Sources

Andersen, Kurt. "What the [Bleep]?! The FCC's Scary New Censorship Crusade Raises the Question: Should the Government Be in the Decency Business at All Anymore?" *New York,* June 5, 2006.

Blake, Bill. "Go Ahead, Steal My Car," *Chronicle of Higher Education,* June 27, 2008.

Boliek, Brooks. "Looking for New Leader in War on Free Speech," *Hollywood Reporter,* May 1, 2007.

Carll, Elizabeth K. "Violent Video Games: Rehearsing Aggression," *Chronicle of Higher Education,* July 13, 2007.

Christian Science Monitor. "Time to Tame TV Violence," May 10, 2007.

Cronley, Jay. "If It's Bore or Gore, TV Gets Bloody," *Tulsa (OK) World,* November 17, 2009.

Current Events. "Game Over: Illinois Governor Says Some Video Games Are Too Violent for Teens," February 18, 2005.

Devereux, Matthew. "The Moral Cost of Video Games," *Christian Science Monitor,* January 7, 2008.

Economist. "Breeding Evil? Defending Video Games," August 6, 2005.

Ferguson, Christopher J. "Video Games: The Latest Scapegoat for Violence," *Chronicle of Higher Education,* June 22, 2007.

Gillespie, Nick. "The FCC Took My Cable Away," *Reason,* April 26, 2007.

Hamilton, Anita. "Video Vigilantes: If Parents Don't Monitor Kids' Access to Violent and Sexual Games, Should the States Do It?" *Time,* January 10, 2005.

Heins, Marjorie. "Politics of TV Violence Returns to Center Stage: FCC's TV-Violence Report," *First Amendment Center*, April 29, 2007. www.firstamendmentcenter.org.

Kerr II, Charles A. "Violent Video Games Reflect What Kids See," *Seattle Post-Intelligencer*, May 7, 2008.

Kopel, Dave. "The Media-Violence Link," *Denver Rocky Mountain News*, November 29, 2008.

Kushner, David. "Off Target: We Shoot Holes Through Studies Linking Violent Games to Aggression," *Electronic Gaming Monthly*, August 2007.

Leaney, Nigel. "Internet Drives Violence," *Community Care*, September 6, 2007.

Los Angeles Times. "Try the On/Off Switch," April 27, 2007.

Lugo, William. "Violent Video Games Recruit American Youth," *Reclaiming Children and Youth*, Spring 2006.

Marche, Stephen. "Are Things Getting a Little Violent? A Thousand Words About Our Culture," *Esquire*, August 2008.

McCormick, Patrick. "Moral Kombat: How Much Should We Worry About the Daily Dose of Interactive, Virtual Murder and Mayhem in Our Kids' Lives?" *U.S. Catholic*, April 2009.

McMasters, Paul. "The Games Censors Play," *First Amendment Center*, October 22, 2006. www.firstamendmentcenter.org.

New American. "Major Media Sensationalizes Mass Shooting Sprees," April 27, 2009.

Paddey, Patricia. "Yes to Christian Values, No to Censorship," *Globe & Mail* (Toronto), March 4, 2008.

Pennington, Gail. "Profanity, Sex, Violence: What's Appropriate on TV?" *St. Louis Post-Dispatch*, March 30, 2008.

Peters, Justin. "Blood, Guts, and Entertainment," *Reason*, February 2006.

Richards Robert D., and Clay Calvert. "Target Real Violence, Not Video Games," *Christian Science Monitor*, August 1, 2005.

Robison, George. "No More Violent Video Game Ads, RTD," *Denver Rocky Mountain News*, March 7, 2007.

Saunders, Kevin W. "Media Industry Should Take FCC Report Seriously," *First Amendment Center*, April 27, 2007. www.firstamendmentcenter.org.

Sirota, David. "Columbine Questions We Still Don't Ponder," *In These Times*, April 17, 2009. www.inthesetimes.com.

Smith, Paul M., and Katherine A. Fallow. "No 'Violence Exception' to Free Speech," *Connecticut Law Tribune*, May 14, 2007.

Sultan, Aisha. "Violent Video Games Not a Safe Outlet for Aggression, Doctor Says," *St. Louis Post-Dispatch*, March 28, 2009.

Tampa Tribune. "FCC Wrong to Tighten TV Censorship," February 25, 2007.

Taylor Jr., Stuart. "Free Speech and Double Standards," *National Journal*, September 29, 2007.

Thierer, Adam. "We Are Living in the Golden Age of Children's Programming," *Progress Snapshot*, July 2009.

Thomas, Mark. "When It Comes to Freedom of Speech We Are Prepared to Defend Only Those Threatened Ideas That We Agree With," *New Statesman*, December 19, 2005.

Walsh, David. "Parents Still the Best Solution to Video-Game Violence," *Syracuse (NY) Post-Standard*, July 5, 2007.

Wilson, S. David. "Don't Blame Video Games for Violence," *Hamilton Spectator* (Ontario), March 20, 2009.

Winter, Tim. "A Commentary on the Federal Communications Commission Report," First Amendment Center, April 27, 2007. www.firstamendmentcenter.org.

Zizzo, David. "An Excess of Crime, War, Gore Raises Stress on TV," *Oklahoma City Daily Oklahoman*, June 11, 2009.

Web Sites

The Lion and Lamb Project (www.lionlamb.org). This site contains information about the effect of violent entertainment on children's behavior.

MediaWise (www.mediawise.org). This Web site provides facts and resources about violence in media, including MediaWise Video Game Report Cards.

SafeYouth.org (www.safeyouth.org) This Web site of the National Youth Violence Prevention Resource Center contains media violence facts and statistics.

Index

Guns
    access to, 31
    decline in teen deaths by,
        20
    mass murders and, 24
    in the media, 25–26, 62

H
Hagelin, Rebecca, 35
Heins, Marjorie, 75
Hill, Edward, 77
Home Invasion (Hagelin), 40
Homicide(s)
    among youth, declines in,
        19–20
    mass, 23–28
    rates, by age group, *19*

I
*In the Matter of Violent
    Television Programming
    and Its Impact on Children*
    (Federal Communications
    Commission), 69, 105
*Interactive Digital Software
    Association v. St. Louis County*
    (2003), 85, 87

J
*Journal of the American Medical
    Association,* 57

K
Kaiser Family Foundation, 91,
    92, 99, 101

*Kendrick, American Amusement
    Machine Association v.*
    (2001), 85–86
Koffler, Daniel, 53
Kronenberger, William, 78, 79
Kunkel, Dale, 60

L
Lasnik, Robert S., 86–87
Lieberman, Joseph, 57

M
*Maleng, Video Software Dealers
    Association v.* (2008), 87
Malvo, Lee Boyd, 48
Martin, Kevin J., 97
Matthews, Karen A., 50
McCormick, Shaun, 45
Mealer, Leslie, 42
Media violence
    contributed to increase in
        mass murder, 23–28
    has harmful effects on youth,
        11–16
    leads to callousness, 29–33
Monitoring the Future survey,
    20
Moore, Devin, 36–37, *37,* 42, 46
Myst (video game), 49

N
National Crime Victimization
    Survey, 20
National League of Cities
    (NLC), 13, 15

National School Safety Center, U.S., 26
National Television Violence Study, 62, 63–64
Nehamas, Alexander, 7
New England Journal of Medicine, 21
Nielsen Media, 99–100

O
Obama, Barack, 22
Office of Juvenile Justice and Delinquency Prevention (U.S. Department of Justice), 20
Olson, Cheryl, 51, 57
Opinion polls. *See* Surveys
Orlet, Christopher, 41

P
Parents
    arguments over video games and, *39*
    TV ratings and, 90, 91
    understanding of TV ratings among, *107*
    use of V-Chip, 90, 97, 101
    views on media violence, *63*
    view on TV regulation, *60, 90*
Parents Television Council, 26, 89
Parr, Jack, 108
Peters, Robert, 23
Peterson, Bart, 11
Pew Research Center, 45

Plato, 7
Policinski, Gene, 104
Politics
    of media violence, 76–77
    of popular culture, 57–58
Polls. *See* Surveys
Pregnancy, 20

R
Rating systems
    television, 91–92
    V-Chip, 101
    video game, *56, 58*
Religion, 24–25
Reno, Janet, 65
Republic (Plato), 7

S
Santorum, Rick, 57
Savage, Joanne, 57
Schaffer, Amanda, 47
Schlafly, Phyllis, 83, *85*
School shootings, 26
Schulenburg, Caroline, 88
Schwarzenegger, Arnold, 81, *81*
Schwarzenegger, Video Software Dealers Association v. (2009), 80
Senate Judiciary Subcommittee on Juvenile Delinquency, 8
Short-Term Psychological and Cardiovascular Effects on Habitual Players, 57
Smoking, 69–70

laws restricting minor's access
to, *79*
may contribute to copycat
violence, 35–40
most popular genres of, *43*
opinions on, *86*
percent of Americans playing,
84
percent of boys/girls playing,
45
positive aspects of, 51–52
prevalence of parents arguing
with child over, *39*
ratings of, 58
should not be blamed for acts
of real violence, 41–46
*Video Software Dealers
Association v. Maleng* (2008),
87

*Video Software Dealers
Association v. Schwarzenegger*
(2009), 80
Virginia Tech shooting (2007),
24, 28, 30

W
Wertham, Frederic, 8
Weyrich, Paul M., 98
Whyte, Ronald, 76, 80
Wolfenstein 3-D (video game),
49
Wollman, Roger L., 84

Y
Yee, Leland, 46

Z
Zogby poll, 91

Picture Credits

© Ace Stock limited/Alamy, 70, 72

AP Images, 31, 37, 44, 55, 81, 91, 95, 102

© Clark Brennan/Alamy, 64

Cengage, Gale, 15, 19, 32, 39, 43, 56, 63, 72, 79, 86, 90, 96, 107

© Leila Cutler/Alamy, 51

© FourT4/Alamy, 106

Hyungwon Kang/Reuters/Landov, 85

Will & Deni McIntyre/Photo Researchers, Inc., 74

© Richard Osbourne/Alamy, 34

Photo Researchers, Inc., 10

©Alex Segre/Alamy, 13

Universal/The Kobal Collection/The Picture Desk, Inc., 27

Miguel Villagran/dpa/Landov, 21

HOW DO BATS SEE IN THE DARK?
Questions and Answers About Night Creatures

BY MELVIN AND GILDA BERGER
ILLUSTRATED BY JIM EFFLER

SCHOLASTIC REFERENCE

CONTENTS

KEY TO ABBREVIATIONS

cm = centimeter/centimetre
g = gram
km = kilometer/kilometre
kph = kilometers/kilometres per hour
m = meter/metre

Text copyright © 2000 by Melvin and Gilda Berger
Illustrations copyright © 2000 by Jim Effler
All rights reserved. Published by Scholastic Inc.
SCHOLASTIC and associated logos are trademarks and/or registered trademarks of Scholastic Inc.

No part of this publication may be reproduced, or stored in a retrieval system, or transmitted in any form or by any means, electronic, mechanical, photocopying, recording, or otherwise, without written permission of the publisher. For information regarding permission, write to Scholastic Inc., Attention: Permissions Department, 555 Broadway, New York, NY 10012.

Library of Congress Cataloging-in-Publication Data

Berger, Melvin.
    How do bats see in the dark?: questions and answers about night creatures / by Melvin and Gilda Berger; illustrated by Jim Effler.
    p.   cm. — (Scholastic question and answer series)
    Includes index.
    Summary: Questions and answers present the habitats and behavior of a variety of nocturnal animals, from cats and kiwis to bats, owls, and foxes.
    1. Nocturnal animals—Miscellanea—Juvenile literature. [1. Nocturnal animals—Miscellanea. 2. Questions and answers.] I. Berger, Gilda. II. Effler, James M., 1956– ill. III. Title.
QL755.5 .B57 2000   591.5′18–dc21   00-023930
ISBN 0-439-22904-9

Book design by David Saylor and Nancy Sabato

10 9 8 7 6 5 4   01 02 03 04

Printed in the U.S.A.   08
First trade printing, October 2001

Expert Readers:
Don Moore, Curator of Animals
Anthony Brownie, Supervisor, Animal Department
Central Park Wildlife Center, New York, NY

INTRODUCTION

Did you know that many animals—bats and owls, raccoons and skunks, lions and leopards, fireflies and cockroaches—wake up around the time you go to sleep?

These night creatures, or nocturnal animals, mostly rest or sleep during the day. But when it's dark, they get busy, usually looking for food.

Very few animals are active only by night or only by day. All night creatures, though, are much more active after dark than they are when the sun is shining brightly.

Night creatures are well suited for the life they lead. They have very sharp senses to help them find their way in darkness. A few have special senses to help them "see" at night by listening for echoes or feeling other animals' body heat. Many are black or gray in color to help them hide and avoid enemies.

Animals prefer nighttime for many reasons. Their daytime enemies can't find them. They can feed on animals or plants that only come out or open in the dark. They don't have to compete with daytime animals for the same food. And they avoid the heat and drying effects of the sun.

How do scientists learn about nocturnal animals? They go out at night and look and listen carefully to what they see and hear. You'll be amazed at what they've discovered about animals that are wide awake when you're fast asleep!

Melvin Berger   Gilda Berger

3

IN THE AIR

How do bats see in the dark?

With their ears! As they fly, most bats make a series of very high-pitched squeaks, or clicks, that are usually too high for us to hear. The clicks strike and bounce off nearby objects and are heard by the bat when the echo returns.

A sound that echoes back quickly lets bats know an object is close. A sound that takes longer to return means the object is farther away. Using sound to find things is called echolocation. Echolocation lets bats see in the dark!

What do most bats eat?

Insects that fly at night. A single brown bat can catch up to 600 insects in an hour!

What do bats eat besides insects?

Fruit, nectar, and pollen from plants; frogs, fish, birds, and other animals; or even blood. There are nearly 1,000 different kinds of bats. Each kind is suited for the life it leads. By looking closely at a bat, you can usually guess what it eats.

Bats that eat insects, for example, have especially large ears to pick up echoes. Plant-eating bats have long tongues to reach deep into night-blooming flowers and lap up the nectar. Vampire bats have special heat-sensing organs to find the blood vessels on their prey. Fishing bats have sharp, hooklike claws to grab slippery fish. And meat eaters have sharp teeth to feed on other bats, rodents, and frogs.

Why do bats fly at night?

A few reasons. Insect-eating bats feast on moths and mosquitoes that come out at night. Plant eaters feed on the nectar of plants that open only after dark. And night is the best time for vampire bats to find the sleeping animals they seek.

Daytime birds also eat insects. Daytime butterflies also suck nectar. By flying at night, bats don't have to compete with these animals for their food.

Lesser long-nosed bat

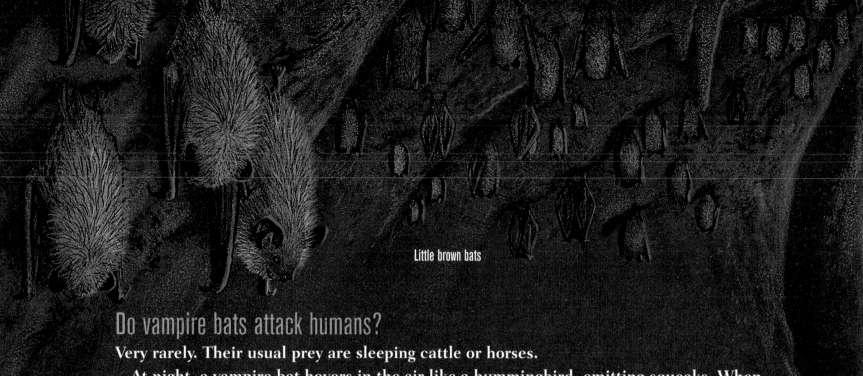

Little brown bats

Do vampire bats attack humans?

Very rarely. Their usual prey are sleeping cattle or horses.

At night, a vampire bat hovers in the air like a hummingbird, emitting squeaks. When its echoes indicate a large animal that's not moving, the vampire bat swoops down. Walking silently, the bat sneaks up on the victim and makes a tiny cut with its sharp teeth. As the blood oozes out, the bat laps up 1 to 2 ounces (28 to 57 g)—a full day's supply. Then away it flies, often before the victim even wakes up.

Are bats bad?

Not at all. In fact, bats help us. Insect-eating bats gulp down huge numbers of insect pests. Fruit-eating bats help spread seeds and pollinate plants. And the manure, or guano, that bats produce is a valuable fertilizer.

Some people think bats are mean because of their strange features, such as giant ears or large nose flaps. But these features are important. Big ears help bats with echolocation. The nose flap lets them direct the sounds they make. Far from mean, bats are gentle and intelligent creatures of the night.

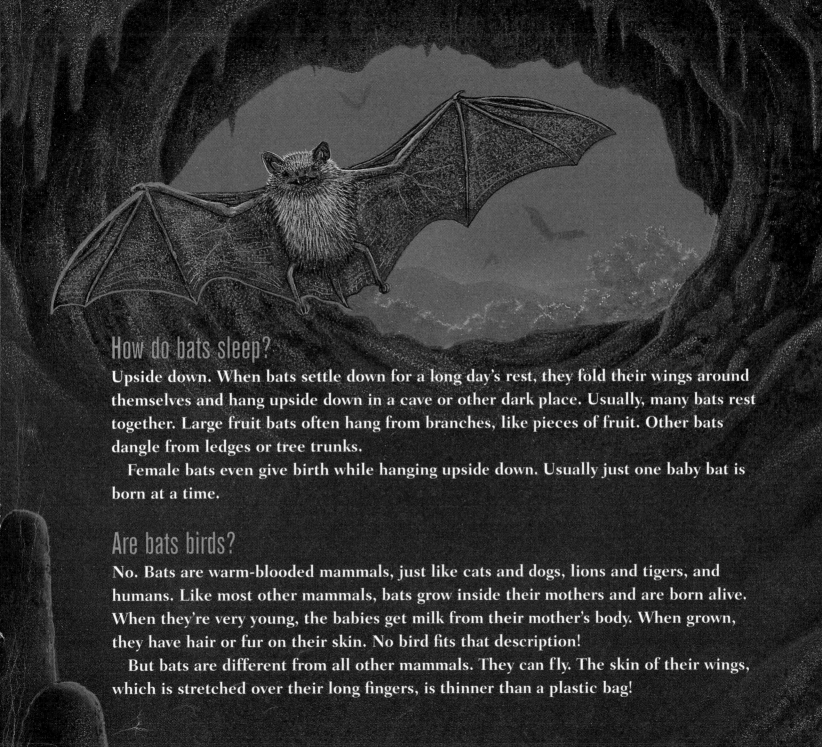

How do bats sleep?

Upside down. When bats settle down for a long day's rest, they fold their wings around themselves and hang upside down in a cave or other dark place. Usually, many bats rest together. Large fruit bats often hang from branches, like pieces of fruit. Other bats dangle from ledges or tree trunks.

Female bats even give birth while hanging upside down. Usually just one baby bat is born at a time.

Are bats birds?

No. Bats are warm-blooded mammals, just like cats and dogs, lions and tigers, and humans. Like most other mammals, bats grow inside their mothers and are born alive. When they're very young, the babies get milk from their mother's body. When grown, they have hair or fur on their skin. No bird fits that description!

But bats are different from all other mammals. They can fly. The skin of their wings, which is stretched over their long fingers, is thinner than a plastic bag!

Which insects often escape bats?

Certain moths. Noctuid (NOK-too-id) moths can hear the high-pitched bat squeaks. As a bat comes close, these moths loop and spiral through the air. This confuses the bat and helps the moths escape.

Arctiid (ARK-tih-id) moths make sounds and clicks that a bat can hear. This disturbs the bat's echolocation, making it hard for the bat to catch them.

Other insects, like lacewings, just fold their wings and drop straight down to the ground when bats are too close. There the lacewings are safe—at least for a while.

Why do moths fly around a light?

They may mistake the light for the moon. Moths navigate by the moon. When they see a lightbulb, they get confused and fly toward it. No doubt you've seen a moth fly around and around a bulb. If the moth gets too near, the heat of the bulb burns its wings, and it dies.

Which moth looks like a hummingbird?

The sphinx moth. This large nighttime moth flies toward flowers that are light-colored or strongly scented. Beating its wings about 35 times a second, the sphinx moth flutters over the flowers like a small hummingbird.

The sphinx moth uncoils its long, tubelike mouth, called a proboscis (pro-BOS-iss), and reaches inside to suck the nectar. In some sphinx moths, the proboscis measures 11 inches (28 cm), which is longer than the moth's entire body!

How do moths find their mates?

By smell. Female luna moths give off a powerful odor into the night air. Male luna moths pick up the smell with their feathery antennae, or feelers. Guided by their sense of smell, the males can find females more than 5 miles (8 km) away!

White-lined sphinx moths

Snowy owl

Are most birds night flyers?

No. Almost all birds are diurnal, that is, active only during the day. Just owls, whippoorwills, and a few other kinds of birds search for food at night.

Can owls see well?

Yes. Owls have gigantic eyes. The central pupil, or dark part of the eye, is extra-large to let in maximum light. This helps the owl see—and catch—small animals in nearly total darkness. Owls see about 10 times better at night than you do.

What makes owls' eyes shine in the dark?

A layer of cells behind the eye, called the tapetum (tuh-PEE-tum). The tapetum works like a mirror. It reflects back any light that enters the eye. The tapetum helps the owl see in very dim light.

Do owls depend more on sight or hearing?

Hearing. The owl's very sensitive ears can pick up the softest sounds. In fact, experts say that a flying owl can hear a sound as faint as a mouse chewing grass under the snow!

In owls, one ear is lower and different in size and shape than the other. This makes the owl very good at finding the exact source of a sound. Also, the owl's face feathers form a disk that reflects sounds to the owl's large ear openings. No wonder owls are such good hunters!

Are owls truly wise?

Not really. Their large eyes make owls look very smart. But experts believe they are not as bright as many other birds. Some say that the owl's big eyes just don't leave enough room for a big brain!

Great horned owl

How do owls hunt?

They look and listen for prey in the dark. When an owl picks up a sound or smell, it silently swoops down toward its target. The owl's soft, fluffy-edged feathers muffle the sounds of its wings.

With sharp, hooked claws extended, the owl pounces on the victim and carries it away. Large owls nab rabbits, squirrels, and skunks. Smaller owls go after insects,

Do owls chew their food?

No. Owls swallow small prey whole. But they rip larger prey into pieces before swallowing. Later, the owls cough up pellets of bone, fur, and feathers that they can't digest.

You may find pellets on the ground under an owl's nest or perch. A pile of pellets found recently contained the remains of about 2,000 mice, 210 rats, 92 blackbirds, and 4 frogs!

Where do owls sleep?

In thick plants and bushes, hollow trees, caves, or old buildings. The owls' dull colors and spotted feathers hide them from their enemies. Despite their name, barn owls also sleep in hollow trees or the rafters of abandoned buildings.

Do all owls "hoot"?

No, the only real hooter is the great horned owl. Other kinds of owls make different noises, from the barred owl's loud barks, to the long-eared owl's whining, catlike cry, to the barn owl's strange-sounding hiss.

In the country, you may hear a shrill whistly sound, running up and down the scale. Some superstitious people don't like this sound. They believe it signals a person's death. But you'll know it's only the cry of a screech owl in the dark.

Striped skunk

Whippoorwills

What bird cries its name all night long?

The male whippoorwill. While perched in a tree, this ghostly night flier sings out its name, "whippoorwill," about 16,000 times between sunset and sunrise! Curiously enough, whippoorwills only call when they are on a perch. They are silent when they fly.

People trying to fall asleep at night may get annoyed at the whippoorwill's cries. But farmers never complain. They're happy to have birds catching the insects that eat their growing crops.

People often call whippoorwills "nightjars" or "goatsuckers." The name nightjar is for the loud, repeated calls that jar people awake. And goatsucker comes from the old and incorrect belief that these night birds suck milk from female goats!

How do whippoorwills catch insects?

By flying with their mouths wide open. Also, around their mouths, the whippoorwills have long, curved facial whiskers that help scoop up bugs in the air.

Where are whippoorwills during the day?

Usually hiding on the forest floor. The whippoorwills' spotted brown feathers blend in with the leaves on the ground. Their excellent camouflage lets them rest safely on the ground from dawn to dusk without being seen.

Which night bird can't fly?

The kiwi of New Zealand. This bird has useless wings. It has neither good hearing nor good sight to help it hunt. But nostrils at the tip of a very long, flexible beak give the kiwi the best sense of smell of all birds. By poking and sniffing in the thick, wet forest floor, the kiwi finds earthworms, insects, and berries to eat. The little hairs around its beak may look strange, but they help the kiwi feel its way in the dark.

Are fireflies a kind of fly?

No. Fireflies, or lightning bugs, are small beetles. They fly together after sunset, each one producing a flashing light in its body. The fireflies make the light with certain chemicals in their bodies that mix together. Nothing burns to make the glow, so there's no heat.

On a summer night, you can see the fireflies' yellow lights flickering over fields and lawns. By day, the fireflies are well hidden in grass or weeds, or hanging motionless on the underside of leaves.

Some people collect fireflies in glass jars. But the light the bugs produce is very dim. So don't count on a jar filled with fireflies to light your way!

Why do fireflies glow?

To attract mates or prey. Each kind of firefly flashes its light off and on in a particular pattern. Since most female fireflies can't fly, they usually perch on the ground or in the bushes and wait. Sooner or later, a male hovers in the air around the female, flashing his special light signal. If the signal is right, the female flashes back—and the male flies over.

Does the firefly's glow also invite enemies?

No. Most firefly enemies, such as birds, frogs, lizards, and spiders, have learned that fireflies are best left alone. Fireflies contain a poison that can kill them.

What are glowworms?

The glowing larvae (LAR-vee) of some fireflies and their close relatives. In time, most glowworms, which look like tiny worms, develop into adult female fireflies.

One kind of glowworm lives in caves. Thousands of them group together. The light they make is bright enough to read by!

Fireflies

Flying squirrels

Do nighttime flying squirrels really fly?

No, they glide. Flying squirrels have extra flaps of
skin along the sides of their bodies. As the squirrel leaps
from a branch, it spreads out its limbs. Wings form, letting the squirrel
glide through the air.

   The squirrel uses its bushy tail as a rudder to steer and keep its
balance. Flying squirrels can reach speeds of about 10 miles an hour
(16 kph) in the air.

Why do flying squirrels glide?

To keep safe. By gliding at night from tree to tree, the squirrels stay clear of enemies on the ground, such as snakes and weasels. Flying squirrels also escape attack by keen-sighted birds of prey, which usually hunt in the daytime.

But being active at night has its own dangers. Many a squirrel misses a branch or crashes into a tree it doesn't see. And night-feeding owls can easily nab flying squirrels in mid-flight.

Where are flying squirrels when it's light outside?

Asleep in hollow trees or abandoned woodpecker holes. The flying squirrels rest in nests lined with dry leaves, feathers or fur, and shredded bark.

Some flying squirrels live in the forests of Asia, Europe, and North America where winters can get very cold. These squirrels sleep rolled into a ball, heads covered with their heavy, bushy tails. On cold days, entire families may huddle together in a single nest to keep warm.

ON LAND

Are cats night creatures?

Yes. Cats' favorite prey are mice, which mostly come out at night. When hunting in dim light, cats open their eyes as wide as possible. With pupils at full size, cats can see about six times better than you! Also, cats have a mirrorlike tapetum behind each eye. The tapetum lets the cat see in almost complete darkness.

Yet cats can also be pretty active during the day. As you know, cats enjoy basking in the warm sunshine. In the bright light, they half-close their eyes to cut down the amount of light that enters. With its pupils closed to just narrow slits, a cat sees about as well as you see.

What other senses help cats hunt in the dark?

Hearing, smell, and touch. A cat's large, sensitive ears pick up all sounds, from the lowest rustle to the highest squeal. A cat's sense of smell is so keen that a newborn kitten can find its mother by scent alone.

The cat feels with its paws and with its long, stiff, and very sensitive whiskers, which are attached to nerves in its skin. The nerves send a message to the brain that tells the cat when it brushes against something—even if it can't see, hear, or smell it!

What sounds do cats make?

None, when hunting. Cats are among the quietest of night creatures. When walking on padded feet, or even jumping from a ledge, they don't make a sound. But when cats fight, it's another story. Two cats screeching at each other at night sound like crying babies or screaming people. During mating season, cats also make lots of noise.

Domestic cat

Lions

Impala

Do lions hunt at night like house cats?

Yes. Lions mostly rest by day and hunt by night. Their main prey are zebras, buffaloes, and antelopes—animals that can easily outrun them.

Lions often hunt in groups. They stalk their prey, much like the way cats stalk mice. When they get to within 100 feet (30 m) of their target, they suddenly leap forward. They either grab a victim with their powerful jaws, or slam it to the ground with their paws.

Lions are not the mighty hunters you might think. They only kill about one out of every four animals they stalk, and they seldom hunt for more than three or four hours a night. Then, it's back to resting. Not a bad life!

Why do lions roar?

Mostly to keep in touch with one another. Sometimes just one lion roars; other times several lions join in a chorus. Experts believe each lion's roar tells the others, "I am here!" This helps members of the pride, or group, stay together, and scares away outsiders.

In the wild, the roar usually starts with one or two softer moans. Then comes the full-throated roar, which you can hear up to 3 miles (5 km) away! The sound lasts about 30 seconds before it fades away to a series of hoarse grunts.

Do leopards hunt like lions?

No. Leopards hunt alone. For this reason, leopards usually go after smaller prey, such as baboons, warthogs, wild dogs, and the young of big animals.

A leopard approaches its prey in an almost snakelike crawl, belly close to the ground. When it is within striking distance, the leopard leaps up and pounces, knocking the prey over. Quickly the big cat buries its two long, sharp fangs in the victim's neck and begins to tear it apart.

After eating its fill, the leopard often carries the leftovers up to a tree. There it drapes itself, and the leftovers, over a branch and takes a nice, long rest.

What night animal is like a big mouse with a pouch?

The opossum. Like mice, opossums are nocturnal animals that have pointed noses and sharp teeth. But like a kangaroo, the female opossum has a pouch on its abdomen for carrying its young.

Female opossums give birth to about 5 to 20 tiny babies at one time. Each is hairless, blind, and deaf at birth and is about the size of a lima bean! An entire litter of 14, for example, weighs less than 1 ounce (28 g) and can easily fit in a soupspoon! The newborns live in the pouch, nursing on their mother's milk.

Do opossums need baby-sitters?

No. Even though the opossum mother is out looking for food every night, her young travel with her.

For the first two months or so, she carries them in her pouch. After that, they crawl out of her pouch and hitch rides on her back for several weeks more. By that time, the nearly full-sized opossums are ready to do their own nighttime food gathering!

What do opossums eat?

Small mice, worms, insects, fruits, roots, and nuts. A particular favorite of small, tree-dwelling opossums is the fruit of the persimmon tree. When persimmons are ripe, some opossums spend the whole night in a tree, stuffing themselves with the fruit.

Who are the opossum's enemies?

Owls, coyotes, foxes, dogs, and cats. When threatened, an opossum lies on its side, unmoving, with eyes closed and tongue hanging out. Since it appears to be dead, predators leave the opossum alone. Now you know the origin of the expression "playing possum," which means pretending to be dead or injured when in danger.

Virginia opossums

What night creatures hunt for food in garbage cans?

Raccoons. Those that live in or near cities will eat almost anything. These "masked bandits" have the amazing ability to break into even the most securely locked trash bins with their long-fingered front paws.

In the wild, raccoons prefer to search near water for frogs, crayfish, and turtles. Those far from water live on berries, nuts, corn, mice, and insects—things not usually found in garbage cans!

Why do raccoons visit the same spots every night?

It's easier than finding new places in the dark. When day breaks, raccoons usually return to the same place to sleep, too. Country raccoons bed down among tree roots or in a hollow tree. If there are no trees, the raccoons sleep in nests they make in high grass. City raccoons make their homes near people's homes—in sheds, drainpipes, or attics.

Raccoons

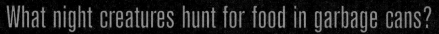

26

Are raccoons endangered animals?

Not at all. In fact, raccoons are growing in number because they can live almost anywhere and eat almost anything. Raccoons adapt well to different habitats—wilderness, farm, or city—and to different climates—from icy cold to tropical.

The raccoons' long gray fur with black tips is camouflage that keeps them well hidden from their enemies. Yet, if attacked, these night creatures become strong, dangerous fighters.

What night creatures are famous for their awful smell?

Skunks. When frightened or under attack, a skunk sends out a horrible-smelling spray from its rear-end scent glands. The most familiar skunk has black fur with bright white stripes from its nose to the tip of its fluffy tail. Other skunks are a solid color or have spots.

Skunks live only in North and South America. They hunt at night in wooded areas for insects, mice, eggs, fruit, and the rotting flesh of dead animals.

What happens before a skunk sprays?

It gives a warning. The skunk may stomp its feet on the ground and give a low hiss or growl. Then, it raises its tail and arches its back. Finally, ZAP!, the smelly, oily liquid shoots out from under the skunk's tail.

How far can a skunk spray?

Up to 12 feet (4 m). The smell chokes nearby animals and they flee. Even worse, the odor can last many days—as people who live in the country know only too well. As bad as the smell is, the spray itself is even worse. If it strikes an eye, the spray can cause burning and temporary blindness. Even one whiff can bring on a stomachache!

Which skunk enemy doesn't mind the smell?

The great horned owl. While hunting at night, this owl does not seem to be bothered by a skunk's spray. Down it swoops to grab the skunk, no matter how strong the odor. Either the horned owl doesn't have much sense of smell—or it just holds its breath!

Giant desert hairy scorpion

Sun spider

Are spiders night creatures?

Some are. Among them are many hunting spiders that chase insects or lie in wait for them, instead of catching them in webs.

All day long, these hunting spiders hide in nests they build out of the silk they spin from special glands in their bodies. When night falls, they leave their nests to search for food. Even though they have eight very small eyes, many of these spiders are nearly blind. To find a victim, they almost have to bump into it!

Do any night spiders live in your house?

Perhaps. The black-and-white parson spider and the grayish mouse spider spend their days in the dark corners of houses or other buildings. At night, they come out to find food. Some evening you might enter a dark room, turn on the light, and see one of these spiders freeze for a second—and then scurry away.

Do spiders have any night relatives?

Yes, scorpions. Many scorpions live in hot lands and avoid daytime activity in the broiling sun. These creatures only venture out at night, when it's much cooler.

In the darkness, scorpions find the spiders and insects they eat mostly by touch. The scorpion stings its prey with the curved stinger at the end of its tail. One shot of the stinger's poison paralyzes the victim and lets the scorpion enjoy its meal in peace!

But even scorpions are not safe from attack. A fight between a camel spider and a scorpion can end badly for the scorpion. The camel spider prances and sways like a boxer to avoid the scorpion's sting. Then it leaps in and holds onto the scorpion's tail until the spider can bite off the stinger.

Do snakes hunt by sight and sound?

No. Many snakes have very poor eyesight and hearing. Their eyes are best for noticing things that move, not for seeing details. Except for objects close to them, everything looks blurry to a snake. And snakes have no earholes. They pick up sound vibrations from the ground.

How do snakes find their prey in the dark?

Partly by body heat. Many snakes, such as the rattlesnake, have heat-sensitive organs located in deep hollows, or pits, between their nose and eyes. The pits allow these kinds of snakes to detect anything that is even a little warmer than the air.

The sidewinder snake is also well equipped with acute heat sensors. Scientists believe that a sidewinder can follow mice and lizards—sometimes right into their burrows— just by sensing the heat of their bodies.

Why does a snake flick out its tongue?

To pick up smells and taste particles in the air. A snake learns the most about its surroundings with its tongue. A snake's tongue helps it track and catch the animals it eats.

Do snakes bite with their tongues?

No. Snakes bite with special teeth called fangs. Poisonous snakes produce poison in glands near their mouths, and tubes carry the poison from the glands to the fangs.

Sidewinder

Granite night lizard

Snowy
tree crickets

Slugs

Earthworms

Are slugs and worms nocturnal creatures?

Yes. These soft-bodied animals need to keep their bodies moist, which means they must stay out of the sun. When night falls, they creep out of their hiding places to search for food. Sometimes, with a flashlight, you can find them in the garden on a warm, damp night. If you're very quiet, you may even hear their faint rustling in dead leaves.

Which night insect has been around longest?

The cockroach. Fossils of cockroaches date back about 250 million years—to the time of the dinosaurs!

   The common cockroach makes its home in food markets, bakeries, restaurants, and people's homes. It belongs to a large family of cockroaches that avoid light and are most active in the dark. Only about ½ inch (1.3 cm) long and a dull tan in color, the common cockroach is not a fussy eater. Food scraps, paper, plants, clothing, dead insects, and just about anything else can make a meal for a cockroach.

Which are the noisiest night creatures?

Tree crickets. Huge numbers gather on trees after dark on warm nights. They produce their loud chirping by rubbing one wing against the other at a rate of about 40 times a second.

   Male crickets chirp most. Experts believe it is how they find their mates. Crickets hear with two small spots, or ears, just under the knees of their front legs.

   A cricket's chirp changes as the air temperature changes. The higher the temperature, the faster the chirps. On a summer night, count the number of chirps you hear in 15 seconds. Add 40 to that number. The sum will give you the temperature in degrees Fahrenheit.

Are frogs night creatures?

Mostly, even though you can see them during the day. Frogs must stay out of the sun, which dries their skin. Like other amphibians, frogs live in water and on land, and breathe with their lungs. But they also take in oxygen through their thin skin. If their skin is not moist, they can't breathe—and they suffocate.

Are all frogs noisy at night?

No, just the males. Both male and female frogs have vocal cords in their throats, just as we do. But in most species, only the males produce the sounds. They do this by pumping air over their vocal cords. To make the sounds louder, the frogs puff up their throats like balloons. They use these calls to attract females. On summer nights you can hear a bullfrog's booming "jug-o-rums" and "br-wums" from up to 1 mile (1.6 km) away.

Where are frogs during the day?

Some are hiding. These frogs keep cool and damp under rotting tree stumps, piles of leaves, mounds of mud, and around wells, docks, or bridges.

Many tree frogs live in tropical rain forests. They hide during the daylight hours by hanging on to the underside of large tree leaves.

Do frogs ever hide at night?

Yes, when the moon is shining brightly. Frogs keep out of sight so their enemies—snakes, raccoons, and skunks—cannot spot them.

Bullfrogs

ies—especially anything that moves. Good eyesight helps frogs capture food and avoid enemies. Frogs' eyes bulge out from their heads. Each eye is like a tiny periscope on a submarine. The bulging eyes let frogs see in all directions—except directly under their noses. In one experiment, scientists placed food right underneath a frog's head. The frog smelled the food, but had to back away to see it.

How do most frogs hunt?

They sit and wait. As soon as a frog sees a moving bug, fish, or small animal, the frog flips out its sticky tongue. SNAP! In a flash, it snags its prey.

A frog will catch and eat almost anything within reach—as long as it is living. Put a hungry frog near a pile of dead, unmoving flies, and the frog would sooner starve than eat them.

When there is no food aboveground, frogs band together and stir up the mud at the bottom of their pond. This helps them find any tiny creatures that might be hiding there. Really desperate frogs will eat anything, anytime—even one another.

Leopard frog

Green frog

How do frogs swallow their food?

With their eyes! After a frog catches a fly or other prey in its mouth, it blinks. This presses the eyeballs down against the roof of the mouth. The roof bends and pushes the food down into the frog's stomach, all in the blink of an eye!

What happens when a frog eats something poisonous?

It throws up its entire stomach. The stomach hangs out the side of its mouth. Then, using its front legs as wipers, the frog brushes the stomach clean—and swallows it back into its body!

American beavers

Blue gills

Where do beavers live?

In rivers, streams, and lakes. Beavers are active day and night, but they're busiest after dark. That's when they collect the twigs, leaves, bark, and roots that they eat. It's also when beavers use their teeth and front paws to cut down trees and build their houses and dams.

Beavers make their houses, called lodges, of logs, branches, and rocks that they hold together with mud. The lodges look like small islands poking up above the water.

Can beavers breathe underwater?

No. They can hold their breath no longer than about 15 minutes. After that, they must either swim to the surface to take a breath or duck into their lodge, which is filled with air.

Are beavers good swimmers?

Yes, excellent swimmers. Beavers paddle through the water, using their webbed feet as flippers. Scientists have clocked them at speeds of about 5 miles an hour (8 kph). When they swim, beavers steer with their stiff, flat tails. They can also use their tails as an extra paddle when they want to put on a burst of speed.

How does a beaver carry a log through water without choking?

It can shut its throat, even when its mouth is open. In this way the beaver carries logs and branches through the water without swallowing a drop!

How do crocodiles spend the day?

Relaxing. Crocodiles usually spend mornings basking in the warm sunlight of the tropical areas where they live. At midday, when it gets very hot, they seek out a cool, shady spot and rest there for a while. After that, it's back to loafing in the sunshine until the sun sets.

American crocodiles

What do crocodiles do after dark?

They look for food. Some stay in shallow ponds or slow-flowing rivers and wait for prey that come to the water for a drink. Others hide in marshes and swamps, ready to attack any animal that wanders by.

A crocodile can gulp down a small animal, such as a turtle, without chewing. But when it catches a big animal, such as a pig, the crocodile rips out hunks of flesh by snapping its jaws shut and flinging its head from side to side.

Are alligators the same as crocodiles?

Not exactly. Alligators have rounded snouts; crocodile snouts are more pointy. Alligators are slower-moving than crocodiles. Also, the alligator's lower fourth tooth is hidden inside its jaw; the crocodile's lower fourth tooth is on the outside of its jaw.

Are turtles night creatures?

No. But one kind, sea turtles, lay their eggs only at night, and for a very good reason: Eggs laid in damp darkness do not dry out as much as eggs laid in the heat of day.

When ready to lay eggs, the large, heavy female sea turtles crawl out of the water. They waddle up on the beach beyond the high-tide mark. With their back flippers, they dig a pit into which they lay 50 to 100 eggs. Finally, they brush back the sand to completely cover the hole. It's usually dawn before they're done and ready to head back to the sea.

When do sea turtle eggs hatch?

Any time of the day or night. But once they hatch, the baby turtles stay hidden in the sand. They wait until it grows dark and the temperature drops. Only then do the baby turtles climb out of their hiding places and crawl as fast as they can to the water. By waiting until dark, the baby turtles avoid the sun and escape gulls and other daytime predators along the shore.

Which night feeders catch baby sea turtles?

Ghost crabs. All day long these crabs hide under seaweed, stones, or in burrows in the sand. But after sunset, they crawl out to look for food.

The ghost crab's eyes are at the end of two long stalks, which it waves around to spot danger. If a crab sees anything menacing, it scurries back into its burrow. Otherwise, it runs sideways along the sand, picking through seaweed and feeding on sand fleas, dead fish, and, of course, newly hatched sea turtles.

Green sea turtles

Ghost crab

Which shark feeds mostly at night?

The hammerhead. Some scientists have traced the daily activities of a group of hammerheads. By day, the sharks swim in circles around underwater mountains, called seamounts. At dusk, the sharks head for their feeding ground, a distance of about 10 to 15 miles (16 to 24 km). All night long, these sharks gulp down tremendous numbers of squid and different kinds of fish.

At dawn, the hammerheads make their way back to the seamounts. Strangely enough, they follow the exact same route going and coming.

What other fish feed mostly at night?

Big, fast-swimming fish, such as tuna, swordfish, and marlin. At night, they come up from the deep water to feed on shrimp and smaller fish that live near the surface. The large fish streak through the upper waters, filling their stomachs with the tasty morsels. Then, at dawn, they descend to the lower depths where they stay until it gets dark again. Sometimes the "commute" from deep water to the surface is hundreds of yards (meters) long.

What kinds of animals are night creatures?

Every kind you can think of—mammals, insects, amphibians, reptiles, birds, and fish. Each has a good reason to prefer the darkness of night over the light of day.

INDEX

About the Authors

The Bergers know firsthand about night creatures. In the summer, they fall asleep to the sounds of owls, crickets, and bullfrogs. In the winter, they wake up to the sight of animal tracks on the snowy ground around their home.

About the Illustrator

Jim Effler finds it interesting that your yard, where you play during the day, could be the habitat for raccoons, bats, and owls while you are sleeping. During the day, Jim shares his yard with his wife, Debbie, and their two daughters, Jenna and Ariana.